# The Handy-Dandy Handbook for Movies in Social Studies

For Amy, Stefania, and Sofia, who gave me the time to put this resource together and the love necessary to do it with a smile.

For Norma, who encourages and has proofread my work since kindergarten.

For all the students, who have enjoyed the zany way content is delivered.

For Lorrie MacGilvray, who renewed my confidence in the belief that anything is achievable.

Text copyright © 2017 by Mike Ward
Cover designed by former student:
Lacresha Holt
Cover digitaly created by:
Tony Martinez
All rights reserved. Published by TLC$^3$ for E.

No part of this publication may be reproduced, stored in a retrieval system, or transmitted in any form or by any means, electronic, mechanical, photocopying, recording, or otherwise, without written permission of the publisher. For information regarding permission, write to Mike Ward, P.O. Box 799, Washington, MI 48094

Library of Congress Cataloging-in-Publication Data

ISBN 978-0-9552409-4-2

Printed in the U.S.A.

# Contents

INTRODUCTION

**Featured Movies: 1492 (PG-13)** ............................................................................................... 1
    Answer Key: 1492 ............................................................................................................... 7

**12 Years A Slave (Rated R) Day 1** ........................................................................................... 8
**12 Years A Slave (Rated R) Day 2** ......................................................................................... 11
**12 Years A Slave (Rated R) Day 3** ......................................................................................... 13
    Answer Key: 12 Years a Slave ........................................................................................ 16

**Lincoln (Rated PG-13) Day 1** .................................................................................................. 17
**Lincoln (Rated PG-13) Day 2** .................................................................................................. 20
**Lincoln (Rated PG-13) Day 3** .................................................................................................. 23
    Answer Key: Lincoln ........................................................................................................ 26

**Avalon** ........................................................................................................................................ 27
    Answer Key: Avalon ......................................................................................................... 31

**The Lost Battalion - Part I (Day 1 - 50 mins)** ....................................................................... 32
**The Lost Battalion - Part II (Day 2 - 50 mins)** ...................................................................... 35
    Answer Key: The Lost Battalion ..................................................................................... 38

**Movie: The Grapes of Wrath** .................................................................................................. 39
    Answer Key: The Grapes of Wrath ................................................................................ 45

**Red Tails (Rated PG-13) Day 1** ............................................................................................... 46
**Red Tails (Rated PG-13) Day 2** ............................................................................................... 49
**Red Tails (Rated PG-13) Day 3** ............................................................................................... 51
    Answer Key: Red Tails .................................................................................................... 53

**Rescue Dawn (Rated PG-13) Day 1** ....................................................................................... 54
**Rescue Dawn (Rated PG-13) Day 2** ....................................................................................... 56
**Rescue Dawn (Rated PG-13) Day 3** ....................................................................................... 58
    Answer Key: Rescue Dawn ............................................................................................. 59

**Forest Gump – Video Activity** ................................................................................................ 60
    Answer Key: Forrest Gump ............................................................................................. 64

**Selma (Rated PG-13) Day 1** .................................................................................................... 65
**Selma (Rated PG-13) Day 2** .................................................................................................... 68
**Selma (Rated PG-13) Day 3** .................................................................................................... 71
    Answer Key: Selma .......................................................................................................... 73

**Mandela (Rated PG-13) Day 1 Long Walk to Freedom** ............................................................. **74**
**Mandela (Rated PG-13) Day 2 Long Walk to Freedom** ............................................................. **76**
**Mandela (Rated PG-13) Day 3 Long Walk to Freedom** ............................................................. **78**
    Answer Key: Mandela ............................................................................................................. 80

**The Butler (Rated PG-13) Day 1** ................................................................................................. **81**
**The Butler (Rated PG-13) Day 2** ................................................................................................. **84**
**The Butler (Rated PG-13) Day 3** ................................................................................................. **87**
    Answer Key: The Butler ........................................................................................................ ..89

**Works Cited:** ................................................................................................................................. **90**

# 1492 (PG-13)

Determined to find a new sailing route to India, Christopher Columbus (Gérard Depardieu) convinces Spanish Queen Isabella (Sigourney Weaver) to finance an expedition. Setting sail with three ships, Columbus quells potential mutinies until the men arrive in North America. After his triumphant return home, Columbus is appointed governor of the new territory, but his dream of a peaceful new world does not fit with nobleman Don Adrian de Moxica's (Michael Wincott) visions of conquest.

*Directions: Use what you know and what you see to respond to the following questions/tasks:*

### Chapter 1

1. As the movie begins, a father and son demonstrate a Renaissance-like curiosity. The father has his son watching a ship. When the ship disappears, the father claims that this proves what theory?
- A. the geocentric theory
- B. the world is flat
- C. the world is round
- D. the Roman Catholic Church is corrupt
- E. none of the choices

2. Why did he want to sail west?
- A. curiosity
- B. to access the riches of Asia
- C. to prove the world is round
- D. to support the church financially
- E. none of the choices

3. How long did the trip take to get to Asia and back if one sailed around the African continent?
A. one month
B. one decade
C. one century
D. one year
E. none of the choices

4. According to the movie, if one spoke out against the church and its beliefs, they would be punished by....
A. hanging
B. burned at the stake
C. sent to a remote island
D. sent to prison
E. none of the choices

## Chapter 2

5. The movie begins in the year....
A. 1491
B. 1492
C. 1493
D. 1494
E. none of the choices

6. If Spain could get to Asia by sailing west, the country would gain wealth. It also promised that they would gain the status of a/an....
A. realm
B. empire
C. religious dynasty
D. of a saint
E. none of the choices

7. The main character in the movie is....
A. the child
B. the priest
C. the pope
D. Christopher Columbus
E. none of the choices

8. Granada was falling out of the hands of what Islamic culture?
A. Moors
B. Mongols
C. Crusaders
D. Byzantines
E. none of the choices

## Chapter 3

9. Christopher meets the queen to ask for her financial support and permission to sail. What was the queen's name?
A. Elizabeth
B. Catherine
C. Mary
D. Isabella
E. none of the choices

10. Was the Columbus request accepted or denied by the queen?
A. accepted    or    B. denied

11. Was Columbus married or single?   A. married    or    B. single

*Chapter 4*
12. What problem was reported to Columbus once the voyage started?
A. the ship was taking on water
B. they were running out of food
C. the crew feared that location could not be calculated
D. illness had taken the lives of many crew members

13. What three ships were mentioned as Columbus was motivating the crew to continue the trip?
A. Pinta, Nina, Santa Maria
B. Mayflower, Sea-Dragon, Hoarse-Fly
C. Sea-Biscuit, Marymount, Merrimack
D. Caravel, Schooner, Cruiser
E. none of the choices

*Chapter 5*
14. Do they eventually find land in this movie?   A. Yes   B. No

15. What was the land called?
A. San Juan
B. Sana Monica
C. San Rio
D. San Salvador
E. none of the choices

16. What word best describes the land they found?
A. desert
B. jungle
C. forest
D. snow covered
E. none of the choices

*Chapter 6*
17. What best describes the first meeting with the Native Americans?
A. it occurred as soon as they reached shore
B. it occurred as they traveled inland
C. it never occurred

18. This period in history is sometimes described as the "Meeting of Three Worlds". You have read that the European explorers had contact with Africans and Asians. What was the third group in this meeting?
A. Australians
B. Japanese
C. Native Americans
D. Dutch
E. none of the choices

19. After exploring the New World for a while, Columbus described the area as...
A. too hot
B. like the biblical location of Eden
C. similar to Europe
D. none of the choices

20. What date was mentioned in this chapter?
A. October 21, 1492
B. October 21, 1592
C. October 21, 1692
D. October 21, 1792
E. none of the choices

21. Columbus mentioned he felt safe around the natives for all the following reasons except....
   A. he adapted to the Indian ways
   B. the natives were peaceful and honorable
   C. he respected their beliefs
   D. he and his men were mistaken for gods
   E. their religion
   AB. none of the choices

*Chapter 7*

22. As time passed, communication became easier because....
   A. a native was able to translate
   B. Columbus learned the language
   C. the native peoples could speak Spanish
   D. none of the choices

23. Some men stayed behind at a fort. The name of the fort was....
   A. La Isabella
   B. La Navidad
   C. La Ferdinand
   D. none of the choices

24. What new product was brought back to Spain and introduced at the first gathering?
   A. Alcohol
   B. Corn
   C. Beads
   D. Tobacco
   E. none of the choices

25. In Spain, the religion recognized "God"; however, the natives had a different god. It was....
   A. Nature
   B. Jesus
   C. Buddha
   D. Muhammad
   E. none of the choices

26. The Spanish were intrigued with the new products and stories but were disappointed with...
   A. the failure of Columbus to find a water route to Asia
   B. the fact that the natives did not believe in Christ
   C. the amount of gold brought back
   D. none of the choices

*Chapter 8*

27. How many ships would sail in the second expedition?
   A. 16
   B. 5
   C. 18
   D. 1
   E. none of the choices

28. In what year did Columbus return to the New World?
   A. 1492
   B. 1493
   C. 1494
   D. 1495
   E. none of the choices

29. What happened to the crew that was left behind on their first visit?
   A. they became part of the native tribe
   B. they disappeared
   C. they were killed and beheaded
   D. they returned to Spain

*Chapter 9*

30. The bell was part of an important construction project. The project, when complete, would establish the most important part of the first city in the New World. What was the most important part?
   A. government style city hall
   B. a store and market
   C. a hospital
   D. a church
   E. none of the choices

31. Who was the architect that planned the city?
   A. Leonardo de Vinci
   B. Pablo Picasso
   C. Christopher Columbus
   D. Queen Elizabeth
   E. none of the choices

*Chapter 10*

32. One of crew suggested that the native population could not handle the farm work. He also suggested that they should bring _____ to complete this work.
   A. Ghazis
   B. Slaves
   C. Moors
   D. Janissaries
   E. none of the choices

33. To establish a new city, Columbus suggests that a certain class of people had to start working. They, of course, did not like this idea. What class did Columbus mention?
   A. the lower class
   B. peasants
   C. royalty
   D. nobility
   E. none of the choices

34. At one point, a character mentions how long the second expedition had lasted. How many years had they been in the New World?
   A. ten years
   B. five years
   C. seven years
   D. one year
   E. none of the choices

35. What event sparked retaliation by the native population?
   A. the chopping off of a native's hand suspected of taking gold
   B. the rude comments made by Columbus
   C. the assassination of the crew left behind
   D. the tribal religion

*Chapter 11*

36. This chapter best illustrates....
   A. the conflicts that occurred between the natives and the Europeans
   B. the internal conflict between Columbus' crew and the natives
   C. the natives becoming familiar with Catholic ways
   D. none of the choices

*Chapter 12*

37. Columbus had a rival. What happened to this individual?
A. Columbus beat him in a fight
B. the rival beat Columbus
C. his rival commits suicide
D. none of the choices

*Chapter 13*

38. What ends chapter 13?
A. an earthquake
B. a volcano eruption
C. a huge storm
D. none of the choices

*Chapter 14*

39. Columbus is accused of ...
A. mismanagement
B. not finding gold
C. forced nobility to work like slaves
D. all of the choices

40. Who told the queen about the failures of Columbus?
A. the priest         D. his wife
B. his rival          E. none of the choices
C. his brother

41. Upon arrival of the new leader in the New World, Columbus finds out that someone else has found the mainland. Who was it?
A. Hernando Desoto – Spanish         D. Mr. Ward
B. Amerigo Vespucci – Italian         E. none of the choices
C. Ferdinand Magellan - Spanish

42. What happened to Columbus when he returned to Europe?
A. he was put in prison         C. he was put to death         E. none of the choices
B. he was treated like a celebrity         D. he got married and resumed regular life

43. Does the queen let Columbus return to the New World?   A. Yes   B. No

*Chapter 15*

44. Did Columbus ever return to the New World?   A. Yes   B. No

## Answer Key: 1492

| Day #1 | Day #2 | Day #3 | Day #4 |
|---|---|---|---|
| 1. C | 12. C | 23. B | 34. E |
| 2. B | 13. A | 24. D | 35. A |
| 3. D | 14. A | 25. A | 36. B |
| 4. B | 15. D | 26. C | 37. C |
| 5. A | 16. B | 27. E | 38. C |
| 6. B | 17. B | 28. B | 39. D |
| 7. D | 18. C | 29. C | 40. A |
| 8. A | 19. B | 30. D | 41. B |
| 9. A | 20. A | 31. A | 42. A |
| 10. A | 21. A | 32. B | 43. A |
| 11. A | 22. A | 33. D | 44. A |

## 12 Years A Slave (Rated R) - Day 1

In the years before the Civil War, Solomon Northup (Chiwetel Ejiofor), a free black man from upstate New York, is kidnapped and sold into slavery in the South. Subjected to the cruelty of one malevolent owner (Michael Fassbender), he also finds unexpected kindness from another, as he struggles continually to survive and maintain some of his dignity. Then in the 12th year of the disheartening ordeal, a chance meeting with an abolitionist from Canada changes Solomon's life forever.

---

Solomon Northup wrote and published his memoir, *Twelve Years a Slave* (1853). The book was written in three months with the help of David Wilson, a local writer and journalist. Published by Derby & Miller of Auburn, New York. In the period when questions of slavery generated debate and the novel *Uncle Tom's Cabin* (1852) by Harriet Beecher Stowe was a bestseller, Northup's book sold 30,000 copies within three years, also becoming a bestseller.

*Directions: Use what you know and what you see to respond to the following questions/tasks:*

start movie at 6:00 mins

1. Is this movie…..
A. fictional or B. factual?

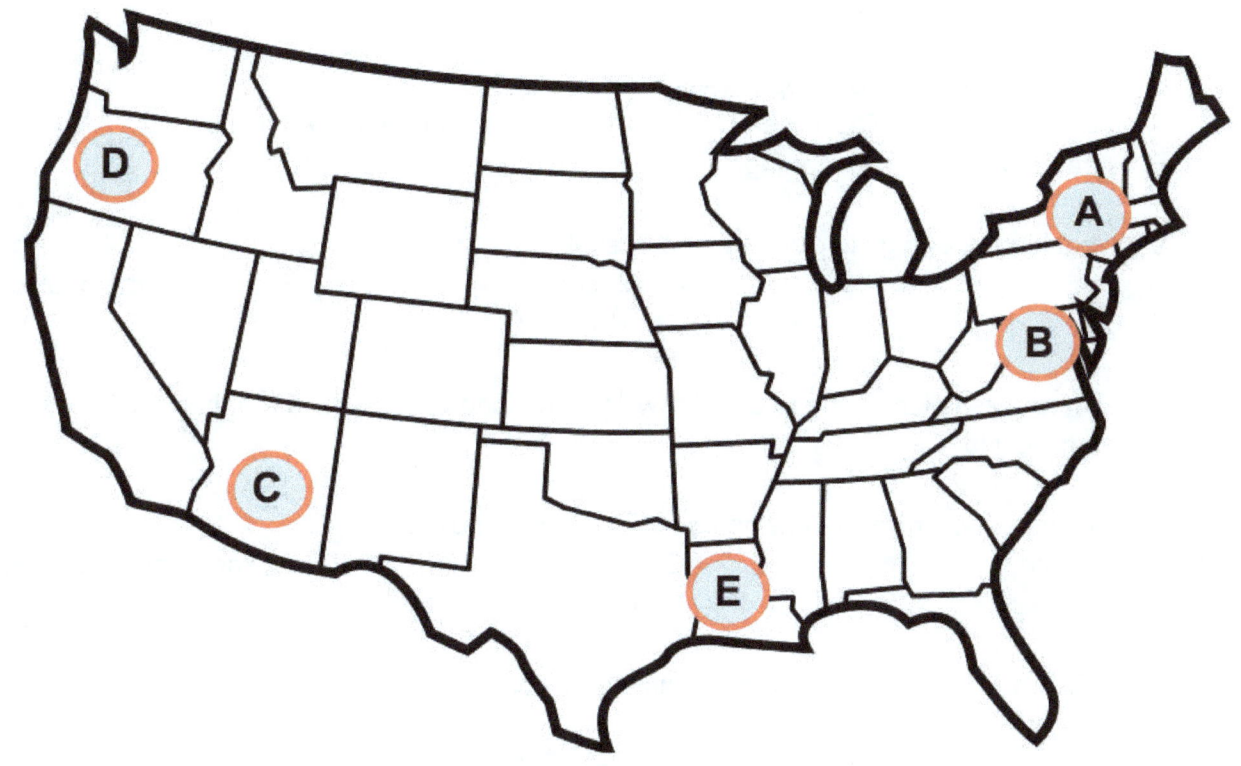

2. What choice on the map above best describes the geographic location as the movie begins?
_____

3. What year is it?
A. 1772  C. 1841  E. none of the choices
B. 1803  D. 1908

_____

4. Using the map above, where is the next stop for Solomon…..
_____

5. After making a lot of money and enjoying a lavish dinner, Solomon finds himself….
A. on a fast path to success   C. back with his wife   E. none of the choices
B. playing more music concerts   D. chained and held captive

6. Solomon could not produce_____to prove that he was a free man?
A. a driver's license   C. enhanced ID   E. none of the choices
B. passport   D. dog tags

7. Solomon's captor convinces him by using torture that he is....
A. no longer a free man
B. a slave from Georgia
C. a runaway
D. not from New York
E. all of the choices

8. How was the group of people transported south?
A. train
B. steamboat
C. plane
D. carriage
E. none of the choices

9. What kind of energy is powering the vessel?
A. coal
B. gas
C. electricity
D. oil
E. none of the choices

10. There was talk of trying to overthrow the crew and escape. Did that happen?
A. Yes  B. No

11. Solomon was given a new name. What was he now called?
A. Terrace
B. Alanzo
C. Jasper
D. Platt
E. none of the choices

(**ALERT at counter 28:50 - scene contains nudity)

12. Eliza's biggest concern was?
A. losing her life
B. losing her children
C. losing her husband
D. losing her mother
E. none of the choices

13. Was Eliza able to keep her children?  A. Yes  B. No

14. Who purchased Solomon (now known as Platt)?
A. Clarence
B. Chapin
C. William Ford
D. Tibeats
E. none of the choices

15. Was Master Ford nice to Platt?  A. Yes  B. No

16. Tibeats went nuts when Platt?
A. was late
B. used the wrong nails
C. followed his directions
D. did not show up for work
E. none of the choices

end day 1 - 47:23

# 12 Years A Slave (Rated R) - Day 2

In the years before the Civil War, Solomon Northup (Chiwetel Ejiofor), a free black man from upstate New York, is kidnapped and sold into slavery in the South. Subjected to the cruelty of one malevolent owner (Michael Fassbender), he also finds unexpected kindness from another, as he struggles continually to survive and maintain some of his dignity. Then in the 12th year of the disheartening ordeal, a chance meeting with an abolitionist from Canada changes Solomon's life forever.

---

Solomon Northup wrote and published his memoir, *Twelve Years a Slave* (1853). The book was written in three months with the help of David Wilson, a local writer and journalist. Published by Derby & Miller of Auburn, New York. In the period when questions of slavery generated debate and the novel *Uncle Tom's Cabin* (1852) by Harriet Beecher Stowe was a bestseller, Northup's book sold 30,000 copies within three years, also becoming a bestseller.

*Directions: Use what you know and what you see to respond to the following questions/tasks:*

1. What made Patsey "queen of the field"?
A.  she could pick over 500 lbs of cotton in a day
B.  she could pick about 400 lbs of cotton in a day
C.  she could pick about 300 lbs of cotton in a day
D.  she could pick about 200 lbs of cotton in a day
E.  none of the choices

2. Is this a correct statement?  Platt could pick more cotton than Patsey
   A.  Yes   B.  No

3. Was Edward Alonzo the new master of Platt?   A.  Yes   B.  No

4. Mistress Epps was angry at her husband Edwin because….
A.  she did not like his drinking habit
B.  she felt he was too hard on Platt
C.  he was not rich enough
D.  she knew that he was intimate with Patsey
E.  none of the choices

5. After the cotton worms destroyed much of the cotton on the Epps plantation, the slaves were….
A.  granted their freedom
B.  sent back to Washington
C.  given a month off to get healthy and relax
D.  sent to a new plantation to cultivate cane (sugar cane)

6. Does Edwin Epps find out about the letter Platt wrote?   A.  Yes   B.  No

7. Is the letter sent?   A.  Yes   B.  No

---

end day 2 - 1:42:05

# 12 Years A Slave (Rated R) - Day 3

In the years before the Civil War, Solomon Northup (Chiwetel Ejiofor), a free black man from upstate New York, is kidnapped and sold into slavery in the South. Subjected to the cruelty of one malevolent owner (Michael Fassbender), he also finds unexpected kindness from another, as he struggles continually to survive and maintain some of his dignity. Then in the 12th year of the disheartening ordeal, a chance meeting with an abolitionist from Canada changes Solomon's life forever.

---

Solomon Northup wrote and published his memoir, *Twelve Years a Slave* (1853). The book was written in three months with the help of David Wilson, a local writer and journalist. Published by Derby & Miller of Auburn, New York. In the period when questions of slavery generated debate and the novel *Uncle Tom's Cabin* (1852) by Harriet Beecher Stowe was a bestseller, Northup's book sold 30,000 copies within three years, also becoming a bestseller.

*Directions: Use what you know and what you see to respond to the following questions/tasks:*

1. After sharing his opinion about those who labor for Edwin Epps, you can see that Bass is mostly like all of the following **except**?
A. a nicer man    C. abolitionist    E. none of the choices
B. a slave owner    D. against slavery

2. Bass sees slaves as a_____; whereas, Epps sees them as _____.
A. property / people
B. good supply of labor / less than human
C. people / property
D. bad investment / wasted capital
E. none of the choices

3. Universal truths are and always will be right or righteous, according to Bass. Bass goes on to predict that the nation will....
A. have a day of reckoning
B. never change
C. witness a day when slaves and whites are equal
D. none of the choices

4. Why did Patsey go to the Shaw plantation?
A. tea and treats
B. soap
C. freedom
D. money
E. none of the choices

(1:48:30) partial nudity

5. Where is Bass from?
A. United States (north)
B. Europe
C. Canada
D. Asia
E. none of the choices

6. Platt asks Bass for all the following **except**....
A. to help escape
B. contact friends in the North
C. secure free papers
D. inform friends about his situation
E. none of the choices

7. Does Bass agree to help Platt?   A. Yes   B. No

8. Who arrives next to call upon Platt?
A. the doctor
B. the wife
C. the judge
D. the sheriff
E. none of the choices

9. His grandson was named........
A. Clarence
B. Chapin
C. Solomon
D. Tibeats
E. none of the choices

Sequencing Events - Use the choices below to put the following events in order as they appeared in the movie:

A. Tricked by two men and enslaved
B. Solomon is reunited with his family
C. Patsey asks Platt to end her suffering
D. Former overseer promises to deliver a letter from Platt
E. Solomon has a comfortable life in Saratoga

10. 1st event
11. 2nd event
12. 3rd event
13. 4th event
14. 5th event

## Answer Key: *12 Years a Slave*

| Day #1 | Day #2 | Day #3 |
|---|---|---|
| 1. A<br>2. A<br>3. C<br>4. B<br>5. D<br>6. E (papers)<br>7. E<br>8. B<br>9. A<br>10. B<br>11. D<br>12. B<br>13. B<br>14. C<br>15. A<br>16. C | 1. A<br>2. B<br>3. B<br>4. D<br>5. D<br>6. A<br>7. B | 1. B<br>2. C<br>3. B<br>4. C<br>5. C<br>6. A<br>7. A<br>8. D<br>9. C<br>10. E<br>11. A<br>12. C<br>13. D<br>14. B |

## Lincoln (Rated PG-13) Day 1

I've rarely been more aware than during Steven Spielberg's "Lincoln" that Abraham Lincoln was a plain-spoken, practical, down-to-earth man from the farmlands of Kentucky, Indiana and Illinois. He had less than a year of formal education and taught himself through his hungry reading of great books. I still recall from a childhood book the image of him taking a piece of charcoal and working out mathematics by writing on the back of a shovel.

Lincoln believed slavery was immoral, but he also considered the 13th Amendment a masterstroke in cutting away the financial foundations of the Confederacy. In the film, the passage of the amendment is guided by William Seward (David Strathairn), his secretary of state, and by Rep. Thaddeus Stevens (Tommy Lee Jones), the most powerful abolitionist in the House. Neither these nor any other performances in the film depend on self-conscious histrionics; Jones in particular portrays a crafty codger with some secret hiding places in his heart.

The capital city of Washington is portrayed here as roughshod gathering of politicians on the make. The images by Janusz Kaminski, Spielberg's frequent cinematographer, use earth tones and muted indoor lighting. The White House is less a temple of state than a gathering place for wheelers and dealers. This ambience reflects the descriptions in Gore Vidal's historical novel "Lincoln," although the political and personal details in Tony Kushner's concise, revealing dialogue is based on "Team of Rivals: The Political Genius of Abraham Lincoln" by Doris Kearns Goodwin. The book is well-titled. This is a film not about an icon of history, but about a president who was scorned by some of his political opponents as just a hayseed from the backwoods. Lincoln is not above political vote buying. He offers jobs, promotions, titles and pork barrel spending. He isn't even slightly reluctant to employ the low-handed tactics of his chief negotiators (Tim Blake Nelson, James Spader, John Hawkes). That's how the game is played, and indeed

we may be reminded of the arm-bending used to pass the civil rights legislation by Lyndon B. Johnson, the subject of another biography by Goodwin.

Daniel Day-Lewis, who has a lock on an Oscar nomination, modulates Lincoln. He is soft-spoken, a little hunched, exhausted after the years of war, concerned that no more troops die. He communicates through stories and parables. At his side is his wife, Mary Todd Lincoln (Sally Field, typically sturdy and spunky), who is sometimes seen as a social climber but here is focused as wife and mother. She has already lost one son in the war and fears to lose the other. This boy, Robert Todd Lincoln (Joseph Gordon-Levitt), refuses the privileges of family.

There are some battlefields in "Lincoln" but the only battle scene is at the opening, when the words of the Gettysburg Address are spoken with the greatest possible impact, and not by Lincoln. Kushner also smoothly weaves the wording of the 13th Amendment into the film without making it sound like an obligatory history lesson.

The film ends soon after Lincoln's assassination. I suppose audiences will expect that to be included. There is an earlier shot, when it could have ended, of President Lincoln walking away from the camera after his amendment has been passed. The rest belongs to history.

Source:   http://www.rogerebert.com/reviews/lincoln-2012

*Directions: Use what you know and what you see to respond to the following questions/tasks:*

1. Is this movie A. fictional or B. factual?

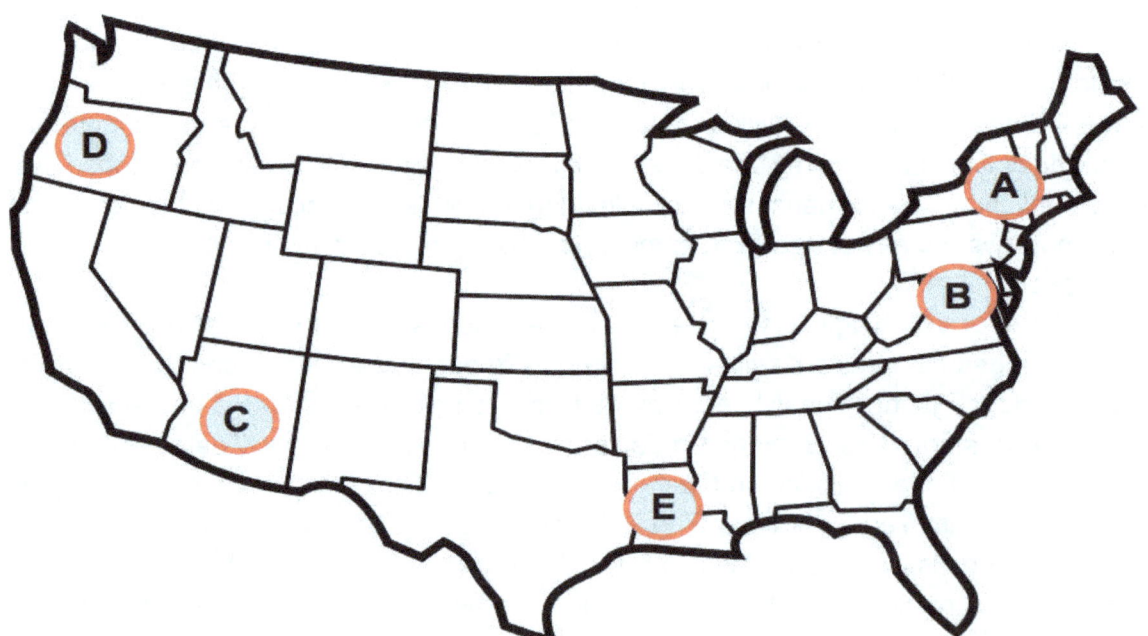

2. What choice on the map above best describes the geographic location as the movie begins?

3. Who were the union troops talking to as the movie started?
A. Abe Lincoln
B. George Washington
C. William Seward
D. Mike Ward
E. none of the choices

4. All the following were discussed at the beginning **except**
A. the Gettysburg Address
B. the Battle of Gettysburg
C. equality
D. Lee's surrender
E. none of the choices

5. In what year does the movie start?
A. 1805
B. 1803
C. 1841
D. 1908
E. none of the choices

6. Abe's wife was very concerned about the passing of which amendment?
A. 10th
B. 11th
C. 12th
D. 13th
E. none of the choices

7. Who was Secretary of State during the Lincoln presidency?
A. Dean Rusk
B. James Buchanan
C. William Seward
D. Ulysses S. Grant
E. all of the choices

8. The 13 Amendment would forever free?
A. the South to make their own laws
B. the slaves
C. rebels
D. the states from emancipation
E. none of the choices

9. Who represented the Radical Republicans?
A. Abe Lincoln
B. Ulysses S. Grant
C. William Seward
D. James Buchanan
E. none of the choices

10. Did the Radical Republicans support abolition?
A. Yes  B. No

11. The men responsible for securing votes for the passage of the 13th Amendment could best be described as.....
A. politicians
B. unlawful
C. lobbyists
D. Democrats
E. none of the choices

---

end day 1 - 44:19

## Lincoln (Rated PG-13) Day 2

I've rarely been more aware than during Steven Spielberg's "Lincoln" that Abraham Lincoln was a plain-spoken, practical, down-to-earth man from the farmlands of Kentucky, Indiana and Illinois. He had less than a year of formal education and taught himself through his hungry reading of great books. I still recall from a childhood book the image of him taking a piece of charcoal and working out mathematics by writing on the back of a shovel.

Lincoln believed slavery was immoral, but he also considered the 13th Amendment a masterstroke in cutting away the financial foundations of the Confederacy. In the film, the passage of the amendment is guided by William Seward (David Strathairn), his secretary of state, and by Rep. Thaddeus Stevens (Tommy Lee Jones), the most powerful abolitionist in the House. Neither these nor any other performances in the film depend on self-conscious histrionics; Jones in particular portrays a crafty codger with some secret hiding places in his heart.

The capital city of Washington is portrayed here as roughshod gathering of politicians on the make. The images by Janusz Kaminski, Spielberg's frequent cinematographer, use earth tones and muted indoor lighting. The White House is less a temple of state than a gathering place for wheelers and dealers. This ambience reflects the descriptions in Gore Vidal's historical novel "Lincoln," although the political and personal details in Tony Kushner's concise, revealing dialogue is based on "Team of Rivals: The Political Genius of Abraham Lincoln" by Doris Kearns Goodwin. The book is well-titled. This is a film not about an icon of history, but about a president who was scorned by some of his political opponents as just a hayseed from the backwoods. Lincoln is not above political vote buying. He offers jobs, promotions, titles and pork barrel spending. He isn't even slightly reluctant to employ the low-handed tactics of his chief negotiators (Tim Blake Nelson, James Spader, John Hawkes). That's how the game is played, and indeed

we may be reminded of the arm-bending used to pass the civil rights legislation by Lyndon B. Johnson, the subject of another biography by Goodwin.

Daniel Day-Lewis, who has a lock on an Oscar nomination, modulates Lincoln. He is soft-spoken, a little hunched, exhausted after the years of war, concerned that no more troops die. He communicates through stories and parables. At his side is his wife, Mary Todd Lincoln (Sally Field, typically sturdy and spunky), who is sometimes seen as a social climber but here is focused as wife and mother. She has already lost one son in the war and fears to lose the other. This boy, Robert Todd Lincoln (Joseph Gordon-Levitt), refuses the privileges of family.

There are some battlefields in "Lincoln" but the only battle scene is at the opening, when the words of the Gettysburg Address are spoken with the greatest possible impact, and not by Lincoln. Kushner also smoothly weaves the wording of the 13th Amendment into the film without making it sound like an obligatory history lesson.

The film ends soon after Lincoln's assassination. I suppose audiences will expect that to be included. There is an earlier shot, when it could have ended, of President Lincoln walking away from the camera after his amendment has been passed. The rest belongs to history.

Source:   http://www.rogerebert.com/reviews/lincoln-2012

*Directions: Use what you know and what you see to respond to the following questions/tasks:*

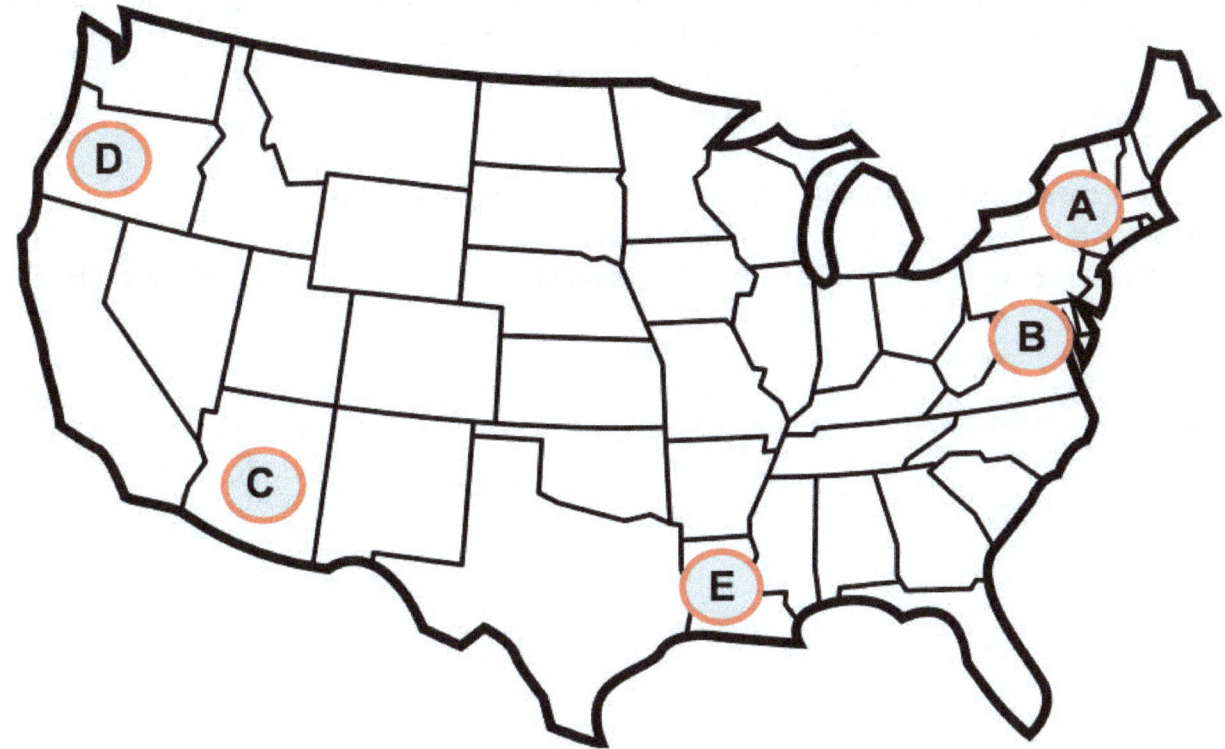

1. What choice is closest to the location mentioned in the movie today?

2. The young boy running around the White House was?
A. a imaginary character   C. a ghost of a fallen soldier   E. none of the choices
B. Seward's nephew   D. Lincoln's son

3. Patronage was mentioned. What choice below best describes a system of patronage?
A. rewarding campaign workers with favors and appointments
B. sponsoring a woman to be married in the 1900s   D. a military term that deals with promotion
C. a political office that was voted on by citizens   E. none of the choices

4. Was anything in the White House illuminated with electricity?   A. Yes   B. No

5. What allowed the battlefield to communicate with the White House?
A. cell phones   C. pigeons
B. pagers   D. telegraph   E. none of the choices

6. What general is shown as the person negotiating with the southern delegates?
A. Robert E. Lee   C. William McClendon
B. Ulysses S. Grant   D. James Hooker   E. none of the choices

7. As President Lincoln sits in the telegraph room with the two young men recounting a story of Euclid's Axioms, what core democratic values were **not** mentioned?
A. Equality   C. Representative Government
B. Justice   D. none of the choices

8. Which member of the Radical Republicans was being questioned?
A. Robert E. Lee   C. William Seward
B. Abe Lincoln   D. Thaddeus Stevens   E. none of the choices

end day 2 - 1:25:05

## Lincoln (Rated PG-13) Day 3

I've rarely been more aware than during Steven Spielberg's "Lincoln" that Abraham Lincoln was a plain-spoken, practical, down-to-earth man from the farmlands of Kentucky, Indiana and Illinois. He had less than a year of formal education and taught himself through his hungry reading of great books. I still recall from a childhood book the image of him taking a piece of charcoal and working out mathematics by writing on the back of a shovel.

Lincoln believed slavery was immoral, but he also considered the 13th Amendment a masterstroke in cutting away the financial foundations of the Confederacy. In the film, the passage of the amendment is guided by William Seward (David Strathairn), his secretary of state, and by Rep. Thaddeus Stevens (Tommy Lee Jones), the most powerful abolitionist in the House. Neither these nor any other performances in the film depend on self-conscious histrionics; Jones in particular portrays a crafty codger with some secret hiding places in his heart.

The capital city of Washington is portrayed here as roughshod gathering of politicians on the make. The images by Janusz Kaminski, Spielberg's frequent cinematographer, use earth tones and muted indoor lighting. The White House is less a temple of state than a gathering place for wheelers and dealers. This ambience reflects the descriptions in Gore Vidal's historical novel "Lincoln," although the political and personal details in Tony Kushner's concise, revealing dialogue is based on "Team of Rivals: The Political Genius of Abraham Lincoln" by Doris Kearns Goodwin. The book is well-titled. This is a film not about an icon of history, but about a president who was scorned by some of his political opponents as just a hayseed from the backwoods. Lincoln is not above political vote buying. He offers jobs, promotions, titles and pork barrel spending. He isn't even slightly reluctant to employ the low-handed tactics of his chief negotiators (Tim Blake Nelson, James Spader, John Hawkes). That's how the game is played, and indeed

we may be reminded of the arm-bending used to pass the civil rights legislation by Lyndon B. Johnson, the subject of another biography by Goodwin.

Daniel Day-Lewis, who has a lock on an Oscar nomination, modulates Lincoln. He is soft-spoken, a little hunched, exhausted after the years of war, concerned that no more troops die. He communicates through stories and parables. At his side is his wife, Mary Todd Lincoln (Sally Field, typically sturdy and spunky), who is sometimes seen as a social climber but here is focused as wife and mother. She has already lost one son in the war and fears to lose the other. This boy, Robert Todd Lincoln (Joseph Gordon-Levitt), refuses the privileges of family.

There are some battlefields in "Lincoln" but the only battle scene is at the opening, when the words of the Gettysburg Address are spoken with the greatest possible impact, and not by Lincoln. Kushner also smoothly weaves the wording of the 13th Amendment into the film without making it sound like an obligatory history lesson.

The film ends soon after Lincoln's assassination. I suppose audiences will expect that to be included. There is an earlier shot, when it could have ended, of President Lincoln walking away from the camera after his amendment has been passed. The rest belongs to history.

Source:   http://www.rogerebert.com/reviews/lincoln-2012

*Directions: Use what you know and what you see to respond to the following questions/tasks:*

1. Did Abraham Lincoln's son (Robert Todd Lincoln) finally enlist to fight in the Civil War?   A. Yes   B. No

2. Lincoln threatened to put Mary in….
A. an mental institution
B. a boat
C. her own house miles away
D. hospital
E. none of the choices

3. What word best describes the backroom wheeling and dealing that takes place in Washington?
A. simple
B. illegal
C. complex
D. straightforward
E. none of the choices

4. At this point in the movie, how many votes stand in the way of passing the amendment?
A. 1
B. 2
C. 3
D. 4
E. none of the choices

5. What date was the vote going to occur?
A. January 1, 1965
B. January 31, 1965
C. January 1, 1865
D. January 31, 1866
E. none of the choices

6. At this point in the movie, it is suggested that a first had occurred. What was it?
A. no vote would occur     C. Abe Lincoln was in audience     E. none of the choices
B. electric lights were used     D. African-Americans were present

7. Does the 13th Amendment to the Constitution pass?     A. Yes   B. No

8. Most_____were for the Amendment; while most
_____were against it?
A. Democrats - Republicans                B. Republicans – Democrats
   (first space   second space)              (first space     second space)

9. Is the statement below  A. true  or  B. false?
As the movie comes close to an end, the director suggests that Thaddeus might be involved in an interracial relationship.

10. Where does the war come to an end?
A. Gettysburg - 1865         C. Richmond - April 1865     E. none of the choices
B. Clinton Township - 1865   D. Appomattox Courthouse - April 1865

## Answer Key:  Lincoln

| Day #1 | Day #2 | Day #3 |
|---|---|---|
| 1. A    | 1. B | 1. A |
| 2. B    | 2. D | 2. A |
| 3. A    | 3. A | 3. C |
| 4. D    | 4. B | 4. B |
| 5. E    | 5. D | 5. E |
| 6. D    | 6. B | 6. D |
| 7. C    | 7. C | 7. A |
| 8. B    | 8. D | 8. B |
| 9. A    |      | 9. A |
| 10. A   |      | 10. D |
| 11. C   |      |       |

## Avalon: Movie Assignment

What makes a family, a family?

Barry Levinson examines the essence of this relationship in his introspective movie Avalon. Almost like looking at someone's photo album, where picture by picture a life story unfolds, this film is a collection of exquisitely crafted scenes that reveal the desires and disappointments of Sam Krichinsky's family as they pursue the American dream.

From the snapshots we learn Sam (Armin Mueller-Stahl) was only able to leave Eastern Europe because his four older brothers pooled together their hard earned wages to pay for his passage. We observe many family circle meetings where contributions are collected to bring over other relatives. We join the gathering of aunts, uncles and cousins for crowded Thanksgiving dinners. And we chuckle at the complexities of multiple generations living under the same roof, next door or across the street from each other.

As the years pass and the clan grows, Sam tries to pass on this history to its youngest members. Despite chiding from his wife (Joan Plowright) about how many times do we need to hear that story? the aging man loves to share the wonder he felt when he arrived in Baltimore on July 4, 1914. Unfamiliar with Independence Day celebrations, the starry-eyed immigrant believed the fireworks were welcoming him to his new home. Although Sam's sentimental tales are largely ignored, his grandson Michael (Elijah Wood) hangs on every word.

But America is not always the Promised Land. We witness this gradual disillusionment through a series of little events. First, an act of violence touches their lives. Then the melting pot philosophy contributes to Sam's son and nephew (Aidan Quinn and Kevin Pollack) changing their last name, sensing no significance in their identity or heritage. Even the blessing of increased financial security and a nicer house in the suburbs only leads to feelings of inequality and greater distance between the kin. When an overlooked minor tradition is taken as a major offence, the final undoing of family ties occurs.

Yet this film is about more than the slow unraveling of the Krichinsky's family fabric. Their plight encapsulates the impact of cultural changes on an entire nation. Some of the subtle influences explored in the movie include the effects of affluence, the introduction of television, and attitudes towards the elderly.

**Directions:** As the movie plays you will learn about a typical immigrant family. It also suggests something about population changes in the 20th century. **I expect you to work alone.** If you miss a day with an excused absence, see me for a makeup assignment. If you are sharing answers during class your grade will be reduced. **Record just your answer choice on the answer sheet.**

1. As the movie begins the main character starts by explaining where he is in the United States. Where is he (city)?
   A. Detroit
   B. Boise
   C. Washington
   D. Baltimore
   E. None of the choices

2. What holiday celebration was occurring as he was walking through the street?
   A. Christmas
   B. New Year's Eve
   C. Thanksgiving
   D. The 4th of July
   E. None of the choices

3. What was this character's name?
   A. William Krichinsky
   B. Sam Krichinsky
   C. Jimmy Krichinsky
   D. Robert Krichinsky
   E. None of the choices

4. Most of the brothers started their working careers as....
   A. Masons
   B. Street Cleaners
   C. Wallpaper Hangers
   D. Politicians
   E. None of the choices

5. What happened during the Christmas holiday?
   A. there was a robbery
   B. Santa came
   C. the children got lost
   D. the salesman got a good paycheck
   E. None of the choices

6. The big Christmas gift that year was a....
   A. Radio
   B. Car
   C. Television
   D. Pop
   E. None of the choices

7. Where did they first live?   A. city   B. suburbs   C. country

8. What issue did Michael have in school (we also have the same issue around here)?
A. missing homework
B. late for class
C. bathroom
D. poor test scores
E. None of the choices

9. One brother (the salesman) had a business idea. He was going to sell....
A. televisions
B. boats
C. radios
D. microwaves
E. None of the choices

10. As the family became more successful, they moved to...
A. the city
B. the suburbs
C. the country

## *End of day 1 – The movie – 50 mins.*

11. What was the typical dinner argument?
A. Feeding the dog
B. Beans
C. politics
D. both a & b
E. None of the choices

12. The mother was very surprised to hear that her brother was still alive (through the Red Cross). The brother had survived the....
A. boat trip across the Atlantic
B. concentration camp
C. Great Plague
D. war wounds
E. None of the choices

13. What was the ethnicity of this family?
A. Polish
B. Italian
C. Jewish
D. Canadian
E. None of the choices

14. The dad, Sam, went crazy when one son and a cousin....
A. committed a crime
B. got married
C. changed their last name
D. stopped working
E. None of the choices

15. As the family business was growing, they decided to guarantee the lowest price in town by...
A. not making profits
B. matching the competition's price
C. selling their old business
D. cutting the quality of the stuff they sold
E. None of the choices

16. The mother-in-law would never....
A. eat a meal at a restaurant
B. drive with the daughter-in-law
C. go back to the old country
D. drink pop
E. None of the choices

17. Was the discount concept for the store a.....
A. success      or      B. failure

18. The family became divided over the issue of....
A. a cut turkey
B. lack of respect
C. distance - they lived too far away
D. a poor meal
E. Choices a,b,c

19. Michael was very surprised when the grandfather and mother....
A. moved out
B. stopped wallpapering
C. drove with the daughter-in-law
D. took a vacation
E. None of the choices

20. The latest business move (that was new at the time) was advertising...
A. in the newspaper
B. on the radio
C. on television
D. on bumper stickers
E. None of the choices

21. What was the family business named?   A. K & K   B. K&K&K   C. K & W

22. The children got into trouble when they...
A. got bad grades in school   B. started a fire   C. neither

## *End of day 2 – The fire – 50 mins.*

Day #3

23. Did Michael admit to burning down the building?   A. Yes   B. No

24. One brother got a job "selling time". What occupation does "selling time" refer to?
A. construction
B. accounting
C. legal
D. education
E. None of the choices

25. After the funeral, one might make the connection that this family was breaking apart. American life had pulled them apart? Is this...... A. True ........   B. False

26. When the family first moved to the U.S., they lived in....
A. a rural area   B. the city   C. the suburbs

27. As the movie ended, part of the family had moved to ....
A. a rural area   B. the city   C. the suburbs

## Answer Key: Avalon

| Day #1 | Day #2 | Day #3 |
|---|---|---|
| 1. D | 10. B | 19. D |
| 2. D | 11. E | 20. C |
| 3. B | 12. B | 21. A |
| 4. C | 13. C | 22. B |
| 5. A | 14. C | 23. A |
| 6. C | 15. B | 24. B |
| 7. A | 16. B | 25. A |
| 8. C | 17. A | 26. B |
| 9. A | 18. E | 27. C |

# Movie Assignment: The Lost Battalion - Part I
# (Day 1 - 50 mins)

## *Background:*
Fact-based war drama about an American battalion of over 500 men which gets trapped behind enemy lines in the Argonne Forest in October 1918 France during the closing weeks of World War I.

The Battle of the Argonne Forest was part of the Meuse-Argonne Offensive planned by General Ferdinand Foch. The offensive called for a three-pronged attack on the Germans at the Western Front. While the BEF and the French Army would attack the German lines at Flanders, the British forces would take on the German troops at Cambrai and the AEF, supported by the French Army, were to fight the German troops at the Argonne Forest.

General John Pershing led the AEF at the Battle of the Argonne Forest while General Henri Gouraud led the French Fourth Army. The attack was launched on September 26, 1918. The combined attack was a success, with the French Fourth Army capturing over five miles of enemy territory and the Americans moving ahead by two miles. By October, the relatively inexperienced American troops needed reinforcements and hence the battle was halted temporarily.

The battle commenced again on October 4, 1918. The attack on the Germans was a commendable one with the Americans making a ten mile inroad by October 17. The French Army had covered over twenty miles of enemy territory and had reached the banks of the Aisne River.

On November 6, 1918, the Allied troops reached Sedan and the American Army halted allowing the French troops to take the city. The armies continued to advance till the end of World War I on November 11, 1918.

## *Outcome:*
The casualties recorded by the Americans at the Battle of Argonne Forest totaled 117,000, while

the French lost 70,000 men and the Germans 100,000 soldiers. The battle was known for the Lost Battalion – 500 soldiers of the Seventy-seventh Division, who fought a brave battle between Bois d'Apremont and Charlevaux against impossible odds. Only about two hundred of them survived the battle.

## *Use what you have learned and the information in the movie to complete the following assignment.*

1. What year did America join the fight known as WWI?
   A. 1914
   B. 1917
   C. 1918
   D. 1941
   E. none of the choices

2. As the movie begins, where is the battle occurring and when?
   A. Battle of Ypres, France (1917)
   B. Meuse-Argonne, France (1918)
   C. Gallipoli, Turkey (1916)
   D. Somme, England (1914)
   E. none of the choices

3. The soldiers were fighting in the...
   A. trenchs
   B. underwater
   C. air
   D. tanks
   E. none of the choices

4. Were airplanes used in WWI?
   A. yes
   B. no

5. Before the war started, in what profession did the commanding officer, Charles White Whittlesey, work?
   A. coach
   B. teacher
   C. priest
   D. lawyer
   E. none of the choices

6. What were pigeons used for during WWI?
   A. food
   B. send messages
   C. pets
   D. surveillance
   E. none of the choices

7. Did WWI occur in the 1900s?
   A. Yes
   B. No

8. What were the men in the trenches nicknamed?
   A. mud punchers
   B. infantry
   C. soldiers
   D. volunteers
   E. none of the choices

9. What word(s) best describes the fighting when the men were asked to leave the trench and attack the enemy?
   A. suicidal
   B. peaceful
   C. violent
   D. both a & c
   E. none of the choices

10. When called, General Alexander stated that the help (also know as the flanks) was right next to the Americans. Was this a truth or a lie?
A. truth          B. lie

11. Were the odds for this mission for or against these soldiers?
A. against              B. for

12. Was the movie depicting the fight on the Eastern or Western front?
A. Eastern        B. Western

13. Who were the Americans fighting with?
A. German                C. French              E. none of the choices
B. British               D. Austrian

14. When they refer to the line being cut, they are referring to a communication line. Since it was cut, what was the fall-back plan to send the message?
A. pigeon               C. Morse code          E. none of the choices
B. cell phone           D. signal

15. What word best describes the circumstances of the featured unit?
A. isolated         B. supported

****End day 1 at 47:10

# Movie Assignment: The Lost Battalion - Part II
# (Day 2 - 50 mins)

## *Background:*

Fact-based war drama about an American battalion of over 500 men which gets trapped behind enemy lines in the Argonne Forest in October 1918 France during the closing weeks of World War I.

The Battle of the Argonne Forest was part of the Meuse-Argonne Offensive planned by General Ferdinand Foch. The offensive called for a three-pronged attack on the Germans at the Western Front. While the BEF and the French Army would attack the German lines at Flanders, the British forces would take on the German troops at Cambrai and the AEF, supported by the French Army, were to fight the German troops at the Argonne Forest.

General John Pershing led the AEF at the Battle of the Argonne Forest while General Henri Gouraud led the French Fourth Army. The attack was launched on September 26, 1918. The combined attack was a success, with the French Fourth Army capturing over five miles of enemy territory and the Americans moving ahead by two miles. By October, the relatively inexperienced American troops needed reinforcements and hence the battle was halted temporarily.

The battle commenced again on October 4, 1918. The attack on the Germans was a commendable one with the Americans making a ten mile inroad by October 17. The French Army had covered over twenty miles of enemy territory and had reached the banks of the Aisne River.

On November 6, 1918, the Allied troops reached Sedan and the American Army halted allowing the French troops to take the city. The armies continued to advance till the end of World War I on November 11, 1918.

## *Outcome:*

The casualties recorded by the Americans at the Battle of Argonne Forest totaled 117,000, while the French lost 70,000 men and the Germans 100,000 soldiers. The battle was known for the Lost Battalion – 500 soldiers of the Seventy-seventh Division, who fought a brave battle between Bois d'Apremont and Charlevaux against impossible odds. Only about two hundred of them survived the battle.

## *Use what you have learned and the information in the movie to complete the following assignment.*

1. Who was General "Blackjack" Pershing?
A. a young German commander
B. General in charge of all American forces
C. commander of the British army
D. the commander of the troops in the Argonne forest

2. Did the artillery fire help or hurt the American soldiers?
A. hurt                B. help

3. Was there some tension between the ethnic groups fighting in the American platoon?
A. yes                 B. no

4. An airplane was used in this film. What was the purpose?
A. bomb the enemy position
B. to show the enemy was superior
C. find the position of the American soldiers
D. none of the choices

5. Was the unit given the offer to surrender by the Germans?
A. Yes                 B. No

6. In the American unit, the second-in-command (George) was career military. Prior to WWI, he fought in the Spanish-American war. Who did he serve under?
A. General Norman Schwarzkopf
B. Major Michael Ward
C. General Pershing
D. Teddy Roosevelt - Rough Riders
E. none of the choices

7. Were flamethrowers used by the Germans?
A. yes                 B. no

8. Did reinforcements ever arrive?
A. yes                 B. no

9. Did any of the Americans survive?
A. yes                 B. no

10. What was collected from the dead soldiers to account for them?
A. dog tags            C. wallets
B. cigarettes          D. fingerprints

11. Are these losses acceptable according to General Alexander?
A. yes  B. no

12. Are these losses acceptable according to Major Charles White Whittlesey?
A. yes  B. no

## Answer Key: The Lost Battalion

| Day #1 | Day #2 |
|---|---|
| 1. B | 1. B |
| 2. B | 2. A |
| 3. A | 3. A |
| 4. A | 4. A |
| 5. D | 5. D |
| 6. B | 6. D |
| 7. A | 7. A |
| 8. A | 8. B |
| 9. D | 9. A |
| 10. B | 10. A |
| 11. A | 11. A |
| 12. B | 12. B |
| 13. C | |
| 14. A | |
| 15. A | |

## Movie: The Grapes of Wrath

The Joad clan, introduced to the world in John Steinbeck's iconic novel, is looking for a better life in California. After their drought-ridden farm is seized by the bank, the family -- led by just-paroled son Tom (Henry Fonda) -- loads up a truck and heads West. On the road, beset by hardships, the Joads meet dozens of other families making the same trek and holding onto the same dream. Once in California, however, the Joads soon realize that the promised land isn't quite what they hoped.

**Directions:** As you watch the movie, answer the questions below. Choose the best answer. They run in order. You need to do this on your own. All questions can be answered by watching carefully. If you choose to collaborate, it could result in points removed or a zero.

---

*Chapter 1*

1. What number is on the truck as the movie begins?
A. 6   C. 53   E. none of the choices
B. 13   D. 83

2. What choice best describes the geographic setting as the movie starts?
A. urban   C. suburban   E. none of the choices
B. rural   D. waterfront

3. As the two characters talk in the truck, the driver learns that the father of the passenger is a?
A. lawyer   C. farmer   E. none of the choices
B. police officer   D. sharecropper

4. As the conversation continues, where do we learn the passenger has been....
A. on vacation   C. at church   E. none of the choices
B. in prison   D. out of the country

5. How long was this character away?
A. 4 years
B. 6 years
C. 10 years
D. 12 years
E. none of the choices

6. For what crime was he there?
A. hitchhiking
B. forgery
C. homicide
D. treason
E. none of the choices

7. What was the passenger's name?
A. Jim Thorpe
B. Tom Joad
C. Tom Headblom
D. Bruce Jenner
E. none of the choices

8. At the time, what "depression" word best describes the preacher?
A. bum
B. retired
C. Hooverville
D. hobo
E. none of the choices

9. What "depression" phrase or word best describes the last scene in this chapter?
A. dust bowl
B. desperate
C) hardboiled
D) crazy
E) none of the choices

*Chapter 2*

10. Were the parents......   A. home   or   B. not home?

11. What character is introduced?
A. Muley Graves
B. Tom Joad
C. the preacher
D. Bruce Jenner
E. none of the choices

12. Where were the parents after they left?
A. vacationing in Europe
B. protesting the bank decisions in Omaha
C. staying with neighbors
D. staying with relatives – Uncle Johns
E. none of the choices

13. Why is everyone leaving (hint - you might have to make an inferences for this one)?
A. the banks were taking back the land (foreclosures)
B. the Dust Bowl caused a reduction in the need for laborers (farmers)
C. modern machinery caused a reduction in the need for laborers (farmers)
D. all of the choices
E. none of the choices

14. Complete this statement by picking the best answer: The driver of the Cat shows us how.....
A. the banks took the land
B. one turns against others to save themselves
C. bleak the situation was during the dust bowl
D. none of the choices

*Chapter 3*

15. Where did the family determine they should go?
A. California  C. Nebraska  E. none of the choices
B. Florida  D. Michigan

16. What lured the family to the new location?
A. family  C. free land  E. none of the choices
B. friends  D. easy transportation (train)

17. What character was the most stubborn about leaving?
A. sister  C. grandfather  E. none of the choices
B. uncle  D. mother

*Chapter 4*

18. How did they finally get this character loaded on the truck?
A. knock him out  C. medicate him with a dose of syrup  E. none of the choices
B. get him drunk  D. tie him up

19. When the Joad family hit the road, they found out that there were….
A. many just like them  or  B. nobody else was in the same situation

20. What character dies in this chapter?
A. sister  C. grandfather  E. none of the choices
B. uncle  D. mother

21. Tom comments that "sometimes government cares more about the dead than the living". This statement would be more consistence with which president?
A. FDR  B. Hoover  C. Truman  D. none of the choices

*Chapter 5*

22. Sharecroppers can best be described as……
A. owners  C. social workers  E. none of the choices
B. businessmen  D. renters

23. One character describes what the future will hold for those going west seeking work. Did his prediction come true?
A. Yes  or  B. No

24. What was the cost of a loaf of bread?
A. $1.00  C. .10  E. none of the choices
B. $2.50  D. .18

25. What state did they enter in Chapter 5?
A. Michigan  C. California  E. none of the choices
B. Arizona  D. New Mexico  AE. both b & c

26. On what road did they travel?
A. Route 66  C. I – 94  E. none of the choices
B. I – 75  D. M - 53

*Chapter 6*

27. What were the Joads warned about as they entered California?
A. their car may not have enough gas  C. the desert is hot
B. their car may not be good enough to cross the desert  D. none of the choices

28. The gas station attendants had a nickname for the Joads, it was....
A. bums  D. Okies  E. none of the choices
B. farmers  C. nomads

29. Do the Joads make it out of the desert?  A. Yes  or  B. No

30. What member dies in this chapter?
A. sister  C. grandmother  E. none of the choices
B. uncle  D. mother

*Chapter 7*

31. How would you best describe the camp they pull into in this chapter?
A. a New Deal Camp  C. a vacation camp  E. none of the choices
B. a tenement camp  D. a Hooverville

32. Mom Joad is put in a tough predicament. What word or phrase best describes it?
A. feed the family or the camp children  C. feed the camp children or the camp counselor
B. feed the family dog or the camp children  D. none of the choices

33. How was the slick businessman manipulating the conditions of the depression to pay the workers the smallest wage possible?
A. get more men than needed  C. lying about wages  E. none of the choices
B. get less men than were needed  D. talking the honest truth  AB. both A & C

34. On what side was the law?  A. the people  or  B. business

35. One more family member disappears in this chapter. It was a common move during the depression. Who disappeared?
A. sister  C. grandfather  E. none of the choices
B. uncle  D. Rosasharon's husband

*Chapter 8*

36. At about every stop, how were the Joads treated?
A. wonderful
B. respectful
C. like family
D. great
E. none of the choices

37. When the Joads finally get work at the Keene Ranch, what must they do?
A. cross a bunch of demonstrators
B. give up all their possessions
C. take a physical exam
D. not talk to anyone
E. none of the choices

*Chapter 9*

38. When the strikers leave, what happens to the wage?
A. it goes down
B. it goes up
C. nothing
D. none of the choices

39. What happens to the preacher in this chapter?
A. he becomes known as the leader of the strike
B. he takes a club to the head
C. he is killed by the guards
D. all of the choices

40. Complete this statement - The popular belief that was working against the unemployed was....
A. they were greedy
B. they were desperate
C. they did not stick together
D. they did not care
E. none of the choices

*Chapter 10*

41. What do the Joads do when they find out that the preacher's prediction was correct?
A. stay
B. go
C. none of the choices

42. What word or phrase best describes the new camp, Farmworkers' Wheat Patch Camp?
A. the same as the last camp
B. worse than the last camp
C. it was a New Deal camp
D. it was a vacation camp
E. none of the choices

43. Who was in charge of running the camp?
A. Department of Commerce
B. Department of Interior
C. Department of Agriculture
D. Department of Recovery
E. none of the choices

44. What were the children all excited about?
A. sinks, showers, and toilets
B. washing machines and dryers
C. automobiles and motorcycles
D. three meals a day
E. none of the choices

45. Tom mentioned a curiosity about a "Red", what was a "Red"?
A. a Native American
B. a communist
C. an anarchist
D. a major league baseball player
E. none of the choices

*Chapter 11*

46. Were the men sent in to start a fight successful?  A. Yes    B. No

47. Who were the police looking for when they entered camp?
A. The Preacher          C. Tom                    E. none of the choices
B. the camp director     D. Grandpa Joad

*Chapter 12*

48. As Tom leaves the camp, one feels that he is now motivated to…
A. call it quits and lay low     C. become active in fixing things     E. none of the choices
B. become a police officer       D. become a preacher

49. Mom Joad explains that they will live forever because….
A. "we are the people"       B. the rich will die out     C. both choices

50. The time period depicted in this movie was….
A. the Great Depression          C. Urban American                E. none of the choices
B. the Roaring 20s               D. the American Industrial Revolution

## Answer Key: The Grapes of Wrath

| Day #1 | Day #2 | Day #3 |
|---|---|---|
| 1. D<br>2. B<br>3. D<br>4. B<br>5. A<br>6. C<br>7. B<br>8. D<br>9. A<br>10. B<br>11. A<br>12. D<br>13. D<br>14. B<br>15. A<br>16. E<br>17. C<br>18. C<br>19. A<br>20. C | 21. B<br>22. D<br>23. A<br>24. C<br>25. B<br>26. A<br>27. B<br>28. D<br>29. A<br>30. C<br>31. D<br>32. A<br>33. AB<br>34. B<br>35. D<br>36. E<br>37. A<br>38. A<br>39. D<br>40. C | 41. B<br>42. C<br>43. C<br>44. A<br>45. B<br>46. B<br>47. C<br>48. C<br>49. A<br>50. A |

# Red Tails (Rated PG-13) Day 1

Like so many others in the late 1930s, the young black Americans who would become known as the Tuskegee Airmen were full of patriotic zeal and eager to serve in the military as the war in Europe and Asia intensified. What set them apart was that they wanted to fight the enemy from the air as pilots, something that black people had never been allowed to do before. Many applied to U.S. Army Air Corps (USAAC) flight training program, but all were initially rejected because of the color of their skin – all branches of the U.S. military were deeply segregated.

In 1940, under pressure from black activists, the press, other political groups and President Franklin D. Roosevelt, the USAAC reversed its position on accepting black flight program applicants. However, the brass was not fully committed to this change and anticipated that the program would fail spectacularly. The Army's decisions about blacks in its ranks were still influenced by a 1925 Army War College report called The Use of Negro Manpower in War. The 67-page report was full of cruel and untrue generalizations about the behavior of black men during wartime and the black race in general.

The new program's cadets were determined to create a record of excellence during their training and future war service so there could be no doubt about their value as patriots and aviators.

---

*Directions: Use what you know and what you see to respond to the following questions/tasks:*

1. Is this movie A. fictional or B. factual?

2. What choice best describes the geographic setting as the movie begins?

3. As the movie starts, the African American pilots suggest that...
A. they are given no important missions
B. they are a key component in the war effort

4. What choice best describes the time frame on this movie?
A. 1920s          C. 1940s          E. none of the choices
B. 1930s          D. 1950s

5. What is the name of the commanding officer?
A. Andrew "Smokey" Salem     C. Joe "Lightning" Little     E. none of the choices
B. Ray "Junior" Gannon       D. Emanuel Stance

6. What character was **not** mentioned in the film?
A. Lightning      C. Junior          E. none of the choices
B. Ray Gun        D. Jackie Robinson

7. Was the military segregated during WWII?   A. Yes   B. No

8. The Red Tails first combat mission was called?
A. D-Day
B. The Battle of the Bulge
C. Operation Shingle
D. Flaming Dart
E. none of the choices

9. Was their job in this mission to provide air cover for a landing?  A. Yes  B. No

10. What color was on the German fighter planes?
A. red
B. blue
C. yellow
D. green
E. none of the choices

11. Do the Red Tails disregard orders when they decided to attack the air base?
A. Yes   B. No

12. Was the first mission a .....   A. success   B. failure

13. What character was hit during the mission?
A. Lightning
B. Ray Gun
C. Junior
D. Jackie Robinson
E. none of the choices


end day 1 - 44:18

# Red Tails (Rated PG-13) Day 2

Like so many others in the late 1930s, the young black Americans who would become known as the Tuskegee Airmen were full of patriotic zeal and eager to serve in the military as the war in Europe and Asia intensified. What set them apart was that they wanted to fight the enemy from the air as pilots, something that black people had never been allowed to do before. Many applied to U.S. Army Air Corps (USAAC) flight training program, but all were initially rejected because of the color of their skin – all branches of the U.S. military were deeply segregated.

In 1940, under pressure from black activists, the press, other political groups and President Franklin D. Roosevelt, the USAAC reversed its position on accepting black flight program applicants. However, the brass was not fully committed to this change and anticipated that the program would fail spectacularly. The Army's decisions about blacks in its ranks were still influenced by a 1925 Army War College report called The Use of Negro Manpower in War. The 67-page report was full of cruel and untrue generalizations about the behavior of black men during wartime and the black race in general.

The new program's cadets were determined to create a record of excellence during their training and future war service so there could be no doubt about their value as patriots and aviators.

---

*Directions: Use what you know and what you see to respond to the following questions/tasks:*

1. Do the Red Tails successfully return from their first combat mission?  A. Yes   B. No

2. Was Lightning the injured pilot?  A. Yes   B. No

3. "Put the bombers first" was the demand for the next mission. Was that true?
   A. Yes   B. No

4. Would the Red Tails get new planes to complete the next mission?
   A. Yes   B. No

5. The officer's club can best be described as….
A. friendly
B. dark
C. a restaurant
D. segregated
E. none of the choices

6. The Red Tails would be flying a new plane. What was the model?
A. A-26 Invader
B. P-38 Lightning
C. P-51 Mustang
D. B-17 Flying Fortress
E. none of the choices

7. The Red Tails were also known as all of the following **except**...
A. African American
B. Tuskegee Airmen
C. pilots
D. part of the 761st
E. none of the choices

8. What pilot went down and was captured?
A. Junior/Ray Gun
B. Lightning
C. Easy
D. Smokey
E. none of the choices

9. How would you rate the performance of the Red Tails?
A. below average
B. average
C. above average
D. poor
E. none of the choices

10. What pilot was injured during the bomber escort and crashed upon the return?
A. Junior
B. Lightning
C. Ray Gun
D. David "Deke" Watkins
E. none of the choices

11. What was the name of the fighter group?
A. 332nd
B. 129th
C. 761st
D. 202nd
E. none of the choices

12. There was talk of a new German weapon, what was it?
A. a submarine
B. a tank
C. a blimp
D. a jet fighter
E. none of the choices

end day 2 - 1:33

# Red Tails (Rated PG-13) - Day 3

Like so many others in the late 1930s, the young black Americans who would become known as the Tuskegee Airmen were full of patriotic zeal and eager to serve in the military as the war in Europe and Asia intensified. What set them apart was that they wanted to fight the enemy from the air as pilots, something that black people had never been allowed to do before. Many applied to U.S. Army Air Corps (USAAC) flight training program, but all were initially rejected because of the color of their skin – all branches of the U.S. military were deeply segregated.

In 1940, under pressure from black activists, the press, other political groups and President Franklin D. Roosevelt, the USAAC reversed its position on accepting black flight program applicants. However, the brass was not fully committed to this change and anticipated that the program would fail spectacularly. The Army's decisions about blacks in its ranks were still influenced by a 1925 Army War College report called The Use of Negro Manpower in War. The 67-page report was full of cruel and untrue generalizations about the behavior of black men during wartime and the black race in general.

The new program's cadets were determined to create a record of excellence during their training and future war service so there could be no doubt about their value as patriots and aviators.

---

*Directions: Use what you know and what you see to respond to the following questions/tasks:*

1. What geographic choice best describes where the next mission would take the Red Tails?

2. Was Lighting getting married?  A. Yes   B. No

3. Were American jets involved in this battle?  A. Yes   B. No

4. Did Lightning sacrifice himself to save Easy?  A. Yes   B. No

5. Despite the loss, was the mission considered a success?  A. Yes   B. No

6. Did the captured soldier (Junior aka Ray Gun) escape from the German prisoner camp?
   A. Yes   B. No

---

Sequencing Events - Put the events below in order as they appeared in the movie:

7. 1st event
8. 2nd event
9. 3rd event
10. 4th event

A. Operation Shingle
B. African Americans are recruited to fight as pilots
C. Assigned to meaningless missions
D. the Red Tails are recognized, honored, decorated for their contributions

## Answer Key: Red Tails

| Day #1 | Day #2 | Day #3 |
|---|---|---|
| 1. B    | 1. A           | 1. A |
| 2. D    | 2. B (Ray Gun) | 2. A |
| 3. A    | 3. A           | 3. B |
| 4. C    | 4. A           | 4. A |
| 5. D    | 5. D           | 5. A |
| 6. D    | 6. C           | 6. A |
| 7. A    | 7. D           | 7. B |
| 8. C    | 8. A           | 8. C |
| 9. A    | 9. C           | 9. A |
| 10. C   | 10. D          | 10. D |
| 11. A   | 11. A          | |
| 12. A   | 12. D          | |
| 13. C   |                | |

# Rescue Dawn (Rated PG-13) Day 1

During the Vietnam War, Dieter Dengler (Christian Bale), a U.S. fighter pilot, is shot down over Laos and taken captive by enemy soldiers. Interned in a POW camp, Dengler and his fellow prisoners (Steve Zahn, Jeremy Davies) endure torture, hunger and illness while they await their chance to escape.

---

*Directions: Use what you know and what you see to respond to the following questions/tasks:*

1. Is this movie A. fictional or B. factual?

---

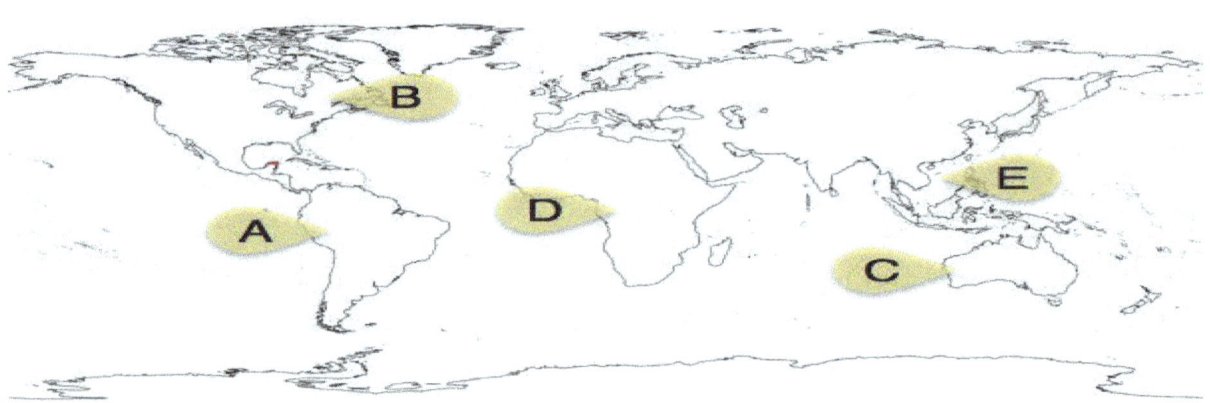

2. What choice on the map above is closest to the geographic location of the movie?

3. What is the first year depicted in the movie?
A. 2000
B. 1965
C. 1908
D. 1964
E. none of the choices

4. What country was the first mission taking them into.....
A. India
B. China
C. Cambodia
D. Laos
E. none of the choices

5. Dieter Dengler is shot down.  Is he captured?   A. Yes    B. No

6. After Dieter refused to sign a document that suggested he was against the war and America's efforts to fight in Vietnam, what best describes how he was treated?
A. he was torchered
B. he was dragged through the village
C. he was hanged
D. he was submerged in water
E. all of the choices

7. What best describes what keeps the prisoners from escaping?
A. the hut is like a jail
B. the jungle
C. none of the choices

8. What made a night escape almost impossible?
A. feet & hands shackled
B. darkness
C. hut was locked
D. extra guards were brought in for the night
E. none of the choices

9. Once the nail was taken, what purpose did it later serve?
A. it allowed them to hang a picture in the hut
B. it allowed them to build a better roof
C. it allowed them to unlock their handcuffs
D. it allowed them to make a knife
E. none of the choices

10. How many prisoners were in the hut?....
A. 1
B. 2
C. 3
D. 4
E. none of the choices

End day #1 48:29

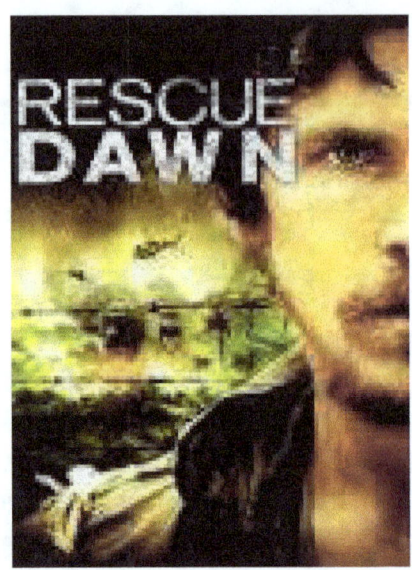

## Rescue Dawn (Rated PG-13) Day 2

During the Vietnam War, Dieter Dengler (Christian Bale), a U.S. fighter pilot, is shot down over Laos and taken captive by enemy soldiers. Interned in a POW camp, Dengler and his fellow prisoners (Steve Zahn, Jeremy Davies) endure torture, hunger and illness while they await their chance to escape.

*Directions: Use what you know and what you see to respond to the following questions/tasks:*

1. The soldiers in the army that visited camp, consisted of......
A. children
B. only women
C. men and women
D. old men
E. none of the choices

2. When was Dieter's birthday?
A. May 22nd
B. April 13th
C. March 19th
D. June 5th
E. none of the choices

3. Does Dieter explain his plan for escape?   A. Yes   B. No

4. The date to escape was decided. It would be....
A. May 22nd
B. April 13th
C. March 19th
D. July 4th
E. none of the choices

5. Was the escape date altered?   A. Yes   B. No

6. How were they able to monitor the guards?
A. by setting their clocks
C. mirror on a stick
E. none of the choices
B. by the way the sun came up
D. the sounding of a horn

7. They were successful in escaping; however, one mistake becomes apparent...
A. name and address printed in the newspaper
C. they have no food to sustain them
B. some of the guards escape
D. the rainy season has not started
E. none of the choices

---

8. Do the men stick together after the escape?    A. Yes   B. No

end day 2 - 1:26:43

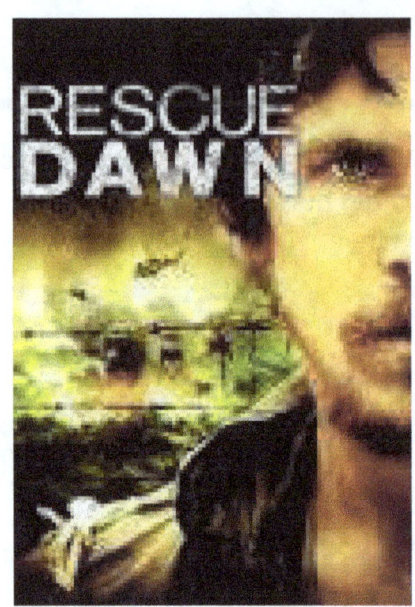

## Rescue Dawn (Rated PG-13) Day 3

During the Vietnam War, Dieter Dengler (Christian Bale), a U.S. fighter pilot, is shot down over Laos and taken captive by enemy soldiers. Interned in a POW camp, Dengler and his fellow prisoners (Steve Zahn, Jeremy Davies) endure torture, hunger and illness while they await their chance to escape.

*Directions: Use what you know and what you see to respond to the following questions/tasks:*

1. The next part of the plan includes….
A. floating to Thailand  C. building a raft  E. all of the choices
B. getting to a river (Big Muddy)  D. floating to safety

2. The men got a brief moment of hope when what appeared?
A. helicopters  C. food left in an abandoned village  E. none of the choices
B. American soldiers  D. the flag of America

3. Did Dwayne survive?  A. Yes  B. No

4. Did Dieter survive?  A. Yes  B. No

5. What best describes the mission Dieter was on?
A. top secret  C. dangerous
B. classified  D. black ops  E. all of the choices

## Answer Key: Rescue Dawn

| Day #1 | Day #2 | Day #3 |
|---|---|---|
| 1. B<br>2. E<br>3. B<br>4. D<br>5. A<br>6. E<br>7. B<br>8. A<br>9. C<br>10. E  (6) | 1. C<br>2. A<br>3. A<br>4. D<br>5. A<br>6. C<br>7. B<br>8. B | 1. E<br>2. A<br>3. B<br>4. A<br>5. E |

Image taken from the public domain

# Forest Gump – Video Activity

*Directions: As you watch this movie, you will notice it touches upon many historic events we addressed in class. You will have to apply what you have learned and what you see to be successful. Good Luck!*

**PART I** (SEQUENCING) - You will have to return to the sequencing portion as the movie begins. Throughout the viewing, place the historic events listed below in chronological order (from oldest to the most recent). You will use 1 - 10 on your answer template. I will get you started by giving you the first answer.

Historic Events:
- A. Governor Wallace blocks integration from happening at the University of Alabama
- B. Forrest is sent to Vietnam
- C. Man lands on the moon
- D. Mention of the KKK and Civil War
- E. Forrest met John F. Kennedy
- AB. JFK and RFK were assassinated
- AC. Forrest met Elvis Presley (aka the King)
- AD. President Nixon resigns the office of president
- AE. President Johnson awards Forest the Medal of Honor
- BC. Jenny lets Forrest sit with her on the bus

11. One of the following geographic places was **not** mentioned in the movie during PART I?
- A. Alabama
- B. Washington DC
- C. Vietnam
- D. California
- E. Michigan

## PART II (MULTIPLE CHOICE)

12. As the movie begins, what kind of shoes are worn by Forrest?
A. Converse
C. Trax
B. Adidas
D. Nike

13. When the movie starts, what year is it? (Hint: Check out the bus)
A. 1961
C. 1981
B. 1971
D. 2001

14. Who was Forrest named after?
A. Nathan Allan Forrest
C. Nathan Regan Forrest
B. Nathan Nixon Forrest
D. Nathan Bedford Forrest

15. Was he named after a real person? You might have to look up the names above to answer this one correctly.
A. Yes
B. No

16. The person he was named after also started the....
A. KKK
C. SNCC
B. NAACP
D. UAW

17. What state did Forrest grow up in?
A. Georgia
C. Pennsylvania
B. Kentucky
D. Alabama

18. What was Forrest's IQ?
A. 105
C. 75
B. 98
D. 86

19. Did Forrest go to.... (Pick one)    A. public school or B. private school?

20. Jenny's dad can best be described as a....
A. loser
C. criminal
B. farmer
D. all of the choices

21. What college did Forrest go to?
A. Alabama
C. Michigan
B. Oregon
D. Miami

22. What beverage was Forrest enjoying at the White House?
A. Coke
C. Mountain Dew
B. Pepsi
D. Dr. Pepper

23. What branch of the military did Forrest join?
A. Navy	C. Marines
B. Army	D. Air Force

24. After basic training, Forrest is sent to….
A. Korea	C. China
B. Russia	D. Vietnam

25. Lieutenant Dan's advice to Bubba and Forrest was….
A. wear dry socks	C. don't salute an officer
B. shoot accurately	D. both A & C

Day #2_____

26. A million dollar wound in the military meant that you…
A. got paid 1 million dollars	C. became an officer
B. got to go home	D. could stay for another year

27. What medal did Forrest get?
A. Purple Heart	C. Medal of Honor
B. Iron Cross	D. Bravery Medal

28. After returning home, Forrest spoke to a crowd at a/an…
A. rally to end the war	C. event in Washington D.C.
B. demonstration to protest the war	D. all of the choices

29. Regarding the war in Vietnam, were the Black Panthers **for or against** the war in Vietnam?
A. for   or   B. against

30. Jenny could best be described as a…..
A. flower child	C. protester of the war in Vietnam
B. hippy	D. all of the choices

31. Who was John Lennon?
A. a talk show host	C. a Vietnam veteran
B. a singer (Beatles)	D. Lt. Dan's cousin

32. Was Hurricane Carmen a real event in history?
A. Yes	B. No

Take a minute to do a search on this one.

33. Is the Bubba Gump Shrimp Company a real shrimp company?
A. Yes	B. No

34. What did Forrest's mom die from?
A. diabetes
C. cancer
B. Lou Gehrig's Disease
D. AIDS

35. The fruit company that Lt. Dan invested in was really...
A. Apple computers
C. a scam and Forrest lost all of his money
B. a fruit company (apples)
D. none of the choices are correct

Day #3_____

36. You have to put the past behind you, before you can...
A. live life
C. play music
B. move on
D. none of the choices

37. What is Jenny sick from?
A. cancer
C. leukemia
B. diabetes
D. AIDS

38. What book did the young Forrest have before entering school?
A. Harry Potter
C. Curious George
B. Blueford
D. Dork Diaries

39. In the movie, which president was not mentioned?
A. Barack Obama
C. Lyndon Johnson
B. Richard Nixon
D. Ronald Reagan

## Answer Key: Forrest Gump

| Day #1 | Day #2 | Day #3 |
|---|---|---|
| Historic Events: | PART II (MULTIPLE CHOICE) | 25. D |
| | | 26. B |
| 1. D | | 27. C |
| 2. AC | 11. E | 28. D |
| 3. BC | 12. D | 29. B |
| 4. A | 13. C | 30. D |
| 5. E | 14. D | 31. B |
| 6. AB | 15. A | 32. A |
| 7. B | 16. A | 33. A |
| 8. AE | 17. D | 34. C |
| 9. C | 18. C | 35. A |
| 10. AD | 19. A | 36. B |
| | 20. D | 37. D |
| | 21. A | 38. C |
| | 22. D | 39. A |
| | 23. B | |
| | 24. D | |

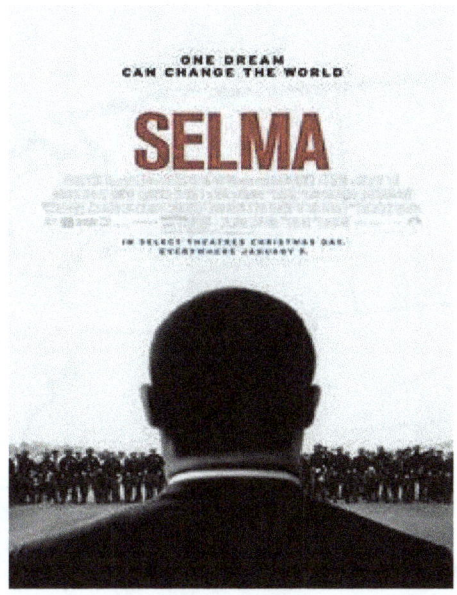

# Selma (Rated PG-13) Day 1

Although the Civil Rights Act of 1964 legally desegregated the South, discrimination was still rampant in certain areas, making it very difficult for blacks to register to vote. In 1965, an Alabama city became the battleground in the fight for suffrage. Despite violent opposition, Dr. Martin Luther King Jr. (David Oyelowo) and his followers pressed forward on an epic march from Selma to Montgomery, and their efforts culminated in President Lyndon Johnson signing the Voting Rights Act of 1965.

---

*Directions: Use what you know and what you see to respond to the following questions/tasks:*

1. Is this movie A. fictional or B. factual?

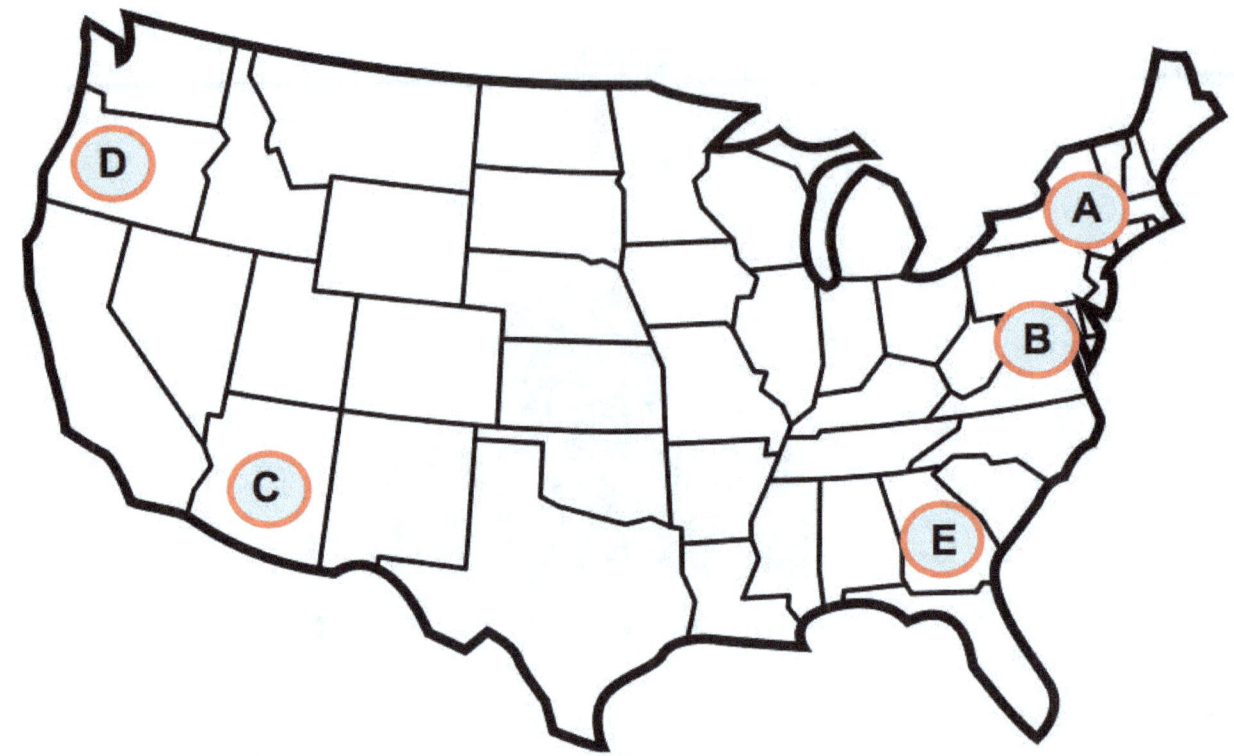

2. What choice on the map above is closest to the geographic location of the movie?

3. What is the first year depicted in the movie?
A. 2000
B. 1968
C. 1908
D. 1964
E. none of the choices

4. Annie Lee Cooper was attempting to…..
A. register to vote
B. get a driver's license
C. join the army
D. bribe a judge
E. none of the choices

5. How were African-Americans kept away from the polls?
A. murders
B. systematic intimidation
C. fear
D. all of the choices
E. none of the choices

6. To serve on a jury, one must be……
A. male
B. registered to vote
C. educated
D. an attorney
E. none of the choices

7. What president met with Dr. King?
A. Kennedy
B. Carter
C. Roosevelt
D. Clinton
E. none of the choices

8. Who was watching Dr. King for the president?
A. Huey Newton
B. Malcolm X
C. Emmett Till
D. J. Edgar Hoover
E. none of the choices

9. Who was Dr. King talking to when he asked to hear the voice of the Lord?
A. Michael Jackson
B. Mahalia Jackson
C. Jesse Jackson
D. Janet Jackson
E. none of the choices

10. The group that Dr. King headed was….
A. SNCC
B. SNL
C. SCLC
D. NFL
E. none of the choices

11. According to the movie, what was necessary to make progress in Selma?
A. Kennedy
B. Eisenhower
C. Johnson
D. drama
E. none of the choices

12. What happened to Dr. King and Ralph Abernathy when they led the protesters to register to vote?
A. they were put in jail
B. the were allowed to register
C. nothing
D. they were turned away
E. none of the choices

---

End day #1 40:46

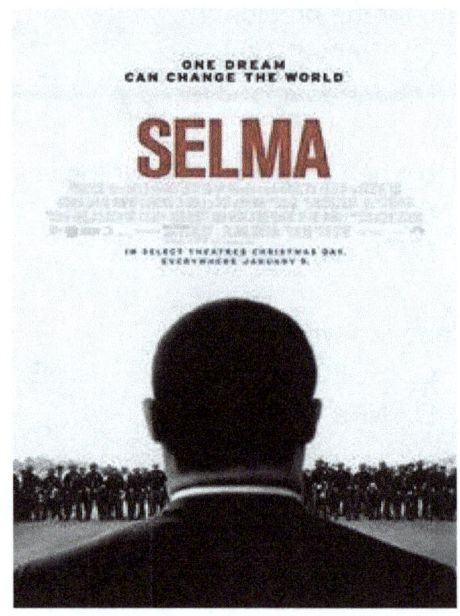

# Selma (Rated PG-13) Day 2

Although the Civil Rights Act of 1964 legally desegregated the South, discrimination was still rampant in certain areas, making it very difficult for blacks to register to vote. In 1965, an Alabama city became the battleground in the fight for suffrage. Despite violent opposition, Dr. Martin Luther King Jr. (David Oyelowo) and his followers pressed forward on an epic march from Selma to Montgomery, and their efforts culminated in President Lyndon Johnson signing the Voting Rights Act of 1965.

*Directions: Use what you know and what you see to respond to the following questions/tasks:*

1. What civil rights leader met with Coretta Scott King?
A. Boris Yeltsin
B. Malcolm X
C. Emmett Till
D. Horace Mann
E. none of the choices

2. Was Martin pleased about his wife's meeting?  A. Yes   B. No

3. With Martin out of town and the cameras of the media gone, how did the police respond to demonstrators?
A. they escorted them through the streets
B. they did nothing to stop the campaign
C. they let protesters demonstrate peacefully
D. they became aggressive and violent
E. none of the choices

4. Read the following passage:

Jimmie Lee Jackson (December 16, 1938 – February 26, 1965) was a civil rights activist in Marion, Alabama, and a deacon in the Baptist church. On February 18, 1965, while participating in a peaceful voting rights march in his city, he was beaten by troopers and shot by Alabama State Trooper James Bonard Fowler.

Was the above mentioned scene portrayed in this movie?    A. Yes    B. No

5. According to Dr. King, who murdered Jimmie Lee Jackson?
A. every white law man who uses a badge to terrorize
B. every white politician who feeds on prejudice and hatred
C. every white preacher who preaches the bible but remains silent before his congregation
D. every negro man/women who resist joining the fight
E. all of the choices

6. According to Dr. King's message at Jimmie's funeral, was America willing to spend millions in Vietnam to promote liberty but lacked the courage to do the same for people at home?
A. Yes    or    B. No

7. All of the options were used to prevent or discourage African-Americans from voting **except**?
A. name and address printed in the newspaper
C. poll taxes
B. voting vouchers
D. show physical fitness
E. none of the choices

8. In the movie, was it suggested that Martin was having an affair (or was perhaps set up to appear as if he was) to discredit his character?    A. Yes    B. No

9. Would you like some extra points?   A. Yes    B. No

10. What big civil rights event was scheduled next?
A. Selma to Montgomery March     C. March on Washington     E. none of the choices
B. Montgomery Bus Boycott        D. lunch counter sit-ins (Tennessee)

11. Is this a correct statement? All civil rights groups/individuals (SNCC, SCLC, Malcolm X) worked together for a common cause.   A. Yes    B. No

12. Read the following passage and analyze the picture below:

   The Selma-to-Montgomery March for voting rights ended in three weeks--and three events--that represented the political and emotional peak of the modern civil rights movement. On "Bloody Sunday," March 7, 1965, some 600 civil rights marchers headed east out of Selma on U.S. Route 80. They got as far as the Edmund Pettus Bridge six blocks away, where state and local lawmen attacked them with billy clubs and tear gas and drove them back into Selma. Two days later on March 9, Martin Luther King, Jr., led a "symbolic" march to the bridge. Then civil rights leaders sought court protection for a third, full-scale march from Selma to the state capitol in Montgomery.

Bloody Sunday: Alabama police await demonstrators at Edmund Pettus Bridge, 1965.
(Photo: Creative Commons/US Dept. of Justice)

Was the scene mentioned above, portrayed in the movie?   A. Yes   B. No

13. Is this an accurate statement? It seems like freedom (in war or in peace) is always tainted in blood.   A. Yes   B. No

---

end day 2 - 1:20:46

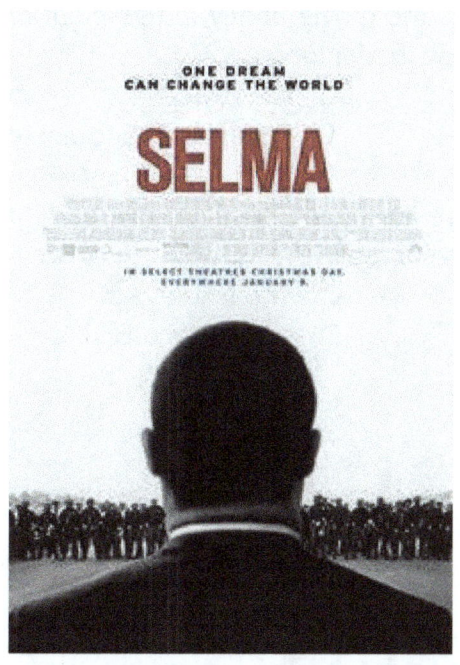

# Selma (Rated PG-13) Day 3

Although the Civil Rights Act of 1964 legally desegregated the South, discrimination was still rampant in certain areas, making it very difficult for blacks to register to vote. In 1965, an Alabama city became the battleground in the fight for suffrage. Despite violent opposition, Dr. Martin Luther King Jr. (David Oyelowo) and his followers pressed forward on an epic march from Selma to Montgomery, and their efforts culminated in President Lyndon Johnson signing the Voting Rights Act of 1965.

*Directions: Use what you know and what you see to respond to the following questions/tasks:*

1. Did Dr. King call off the second march?    A. Yes    B. No

2. What best describes the second march?
A. made it to Montgomery            C. smaller than first    E. none of the choices
B. met with violence & aggression   D. turn around

3. Does a third march have the approval of the court system?  A. Yes    B. No

4. Who was the Governor of Alabama?
A. Edmund Pettus              C. Jimmy Johnson          E. none of the choices
B. Orville Faubus             D. George Wallace

5. According to President Johnson, he would propose legislation to solve a(n)?
A. southern problem           C. American problem
B. Alabama problem            D. nothern problem         E. none of the choices

6. Ask your teacher to pause the movie briefly at this point please.  What happened to Viola Liuzzo shortly after the speech in Montgomery?
A. was murdered
B. drove home
C. was elected
D. became an acclaimed author
E. none of the choices

7. Ask your teacher to pause the movie briefly at this point please.  What piece of legislation made the President's promise, a reality?
A. Voting Rights Act of 1965
B. 13th Amendment
C. The Patriot Act
D. the Wallace Bill
E. none of the choices

## Answer Key: Selma

| Key for Day #1 | Key for Day #2 | Key for Day #3 |
|---|---|---|
| 1. B<br>2. E<br>3. D<br>4. A<br>5. D<br>6. B<br>7. E<br>8. D<br>9. B<br>10. C<br>11. D<br>12. A | 1. B<br>2. B<br>3. D<br>4. A<br>5. E<br>6. A<br>7. D<br>8. A<br>9. A<br>10. A<br>11. B<br>12. A<br>13. A | 1. B<br>2. D<br>3. A<br>4. D<br>5. C<br>6. A<br>7. A |

# Mandela (Rated PG-13) Day 1

The remarkable life of South African revolutionary, president and world icon Nelson Mandela (Idris Elba) takes center stage. Though he had humble beginnings as a herd boy in a rural village, Mandela became involved in the anti-apartheid movement and co-founded the African National Congress Youth League. His activities eventually led to his imprisonment on Robben Island from 1964 to 1990. In 1994, Mandela became the first president of democratic South Africa.

*Directions: Use what you know and what you see to respond to the following questions/tasks:*

1. Is this movie A. fictional or B. factual?

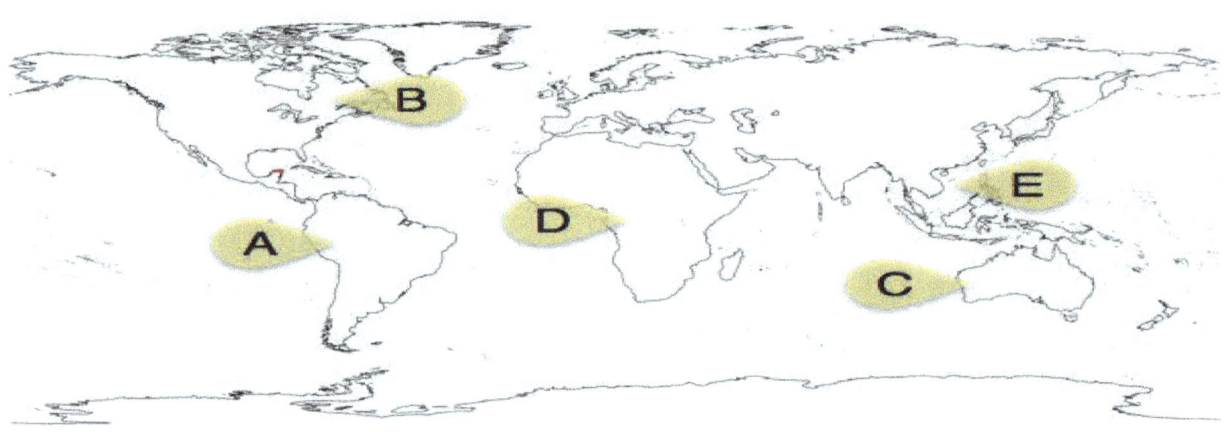

2. What choice on the map above is closest to the geographic location of the movie?

3. The ritual that starts the movie pertains to becoming a?
A. lawyer
B. man
C. warrior
D. tribal scribe
E. none of the choices

4. When translated, Nelson's name was…..
A. lazy
B. leader
C. troublemaker
D. the judge
E. none of the choices

5. What year marks the beginning of the movie?
A. 1962
B. 1942
C. 1982
D. 1862
E. none of the choices

6. What was Nelson's profession?
A. a judge
B. an officer
C. a doctor
D. an attorney
E. none of the choices

7. What did the law state regarding relationships?
A. you can only have relations with those of opposite gender
B. you can only have relations with those of your own race
C. you can only have relations with those of the same religion
D. you can only have relations with those of the same village
E. none of the choices

8. How many times was Nelson married?
A. 1
B. 2
C. 3
D. 4
E. none of the choices

9. Read this passage:

> The Sharpeville massacre was a turning point in South African history. On March 21, 1960, without warning, South African police at Sharpeville, an African township of Vereeniging, south of Johannesburg, shot into a crowd of about 5,000 unarmed protesters, killing at least 69 people – many of them shot in the back – and wounding more than 200.

Was this event depicted in the movie?   A. Yes    B. No

10. What motivates Nelson?
A. freedom
B. violence
C. justice
D. money
E. none of the choices

End day #1 40:08

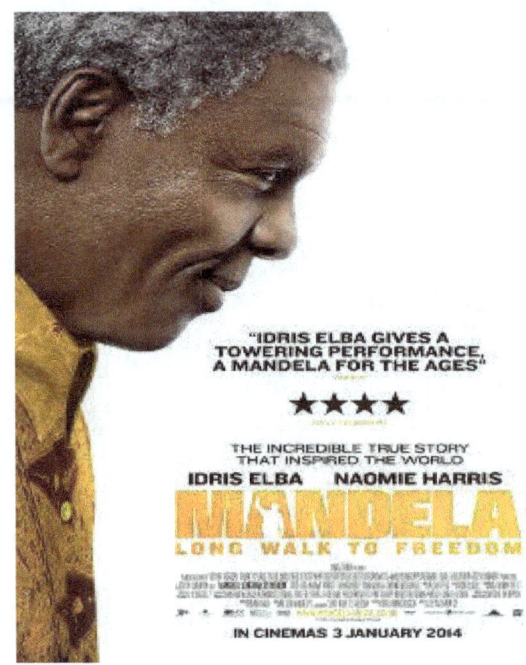

# Mandela (Rated PG-13) Day 2

The remarkable life of South African revolutionary, president and world icon Nelson Mandela (Idris Elba) takes center stage. Though he had humble beginnings as a herd boy in a rural village, Mandela became involved in the anti-apartheid movement and co-founded the African National Congress Youth League. His activities eventually led to his imprisonment on Robben Island from 1964 to 1990. In 1994, Mandela became the first president of democratic South Africa.

---

*Directions: Use what you know and what you see to respond to the following questions/tasks:*

---

1. Did the law finally find and catch up with Nelson?   A. Yes   B. No

2. Does Nelson represent the African National Congress (ANC)?   A. Yes   B. No

3. Martin and others avoid the death penalty; however, they are....
A. sentenced to hard labor
B. set free
E. none of the choices
C. sent to another country
D. asked to pledge forgiveness

4. When the plane lands on Robben Island, what is the year?
A. 1962
C. 1964
E. none of the choices
B. 1942
D. 1873

5. What was the first demand of Mandela's group?
A. long pants
B. clean cells
C. washed clothes
D. more mail
E. all of the choices

6. Was Winnie, the wife of Nelson, left alone?
A. Yes   B. No

7. What year does Winnie leave solitary confinement and how long had she been there?
A. 1967 / 14 month
C. 1970 / 16 month
E. none of the choices
B. 1942 / 12 month
D. 1873 / 8 month

8. What year were the prisoners moved?
A. 1982
C. 1964
E. none of the choices
B. 1942
D. 1873

9. Would you describe the conditions?   A. The Same   B. Improved   C. Worse

---

end day 2 - 1:30:00

# Mandela (Rated PG-13) Day 3

The remarkable life of South African revolutionary, president and world icon Nelson Mandela (Idris Elba) takes center stage. Though he had humble beginnings as a herd boy in a rural village, Mandela became involved in the anti-apartheid movement and co-founded the African National Congress Youth League. His activities eventually led to his imprisonment on Robben Island from 1964 to 1990. In 1994, Mandela became the first president of democratic South Africa.

---

*Directions: Use what you know and what you see to respond to the following questions/tasks:*

---

1. How long had it been since Nelson touched his wife?
A. 5 years            C. 21 years           E. none of the choices
B. 12 years           D. 32 years

2. Does Nelson accept the offer that would grant him his freedom?   A. Yes    B. No

3. When Nelson begins to negotiate with the government, is he separated from his colleagues?
A. Yes   B. No

4. Were his colleagues pleased with this decision?   A. Yes    B. No

5. When was Nelson Mandela finally released?
A. March 19th, 1989     C. June 6th, 1941
B. April 7th, 2001     D. May 21 1972     E. none of the choices

6. Do Nelson and Winnie share different views concerning how to bring about freedom?
A. Yes    B. No

7. Despite the urge to fight and continue the violence, Nelson publically promotes _____ and tells his people to_____.

A. peace / vote     C. forgiveness / get even     E. none of the choices
B. violence / get more guns     D. President de Klerk / back off

8. Election day would be held on:
A. March 19th, 1989     C. June 6th, 1941
B. April 27th, 1994     D. May 21 1972     E. none of the choices

9. What comes more naturally to the human heart?   A. Hate   or   B. Love

10. You might have to look this one up. Did Nelson become president of South Africa?
A. Yes    B. No

## Answer Key: Mandela

| Day #1 | Day #2 | Day #3 |
|---|---|---|
| 1. B  | 1. A | 1. C |
| 2. D  | 2. A | 2. B |
| 3. B  | 3. E | 3. A |
| 4. C  | 4. C | 4. B |
| 5. B  | 5. A | 5. E  (Feb 11, 1990) |
| 6. D  | 6. B | 6. A |
| 7. B  | 7. C | 7. A |
| 8. B  | 8. A | 8. B |
| 9. A  | 9. B | 9. B |
| 10. A |      | 10. A |

# The Butler (Rated PG-13) Day 1

After leaving the South as a young man and finding employment at an elite hotel in Washington, D.C., Cecil Gaines (Forest Whitaker) gets the opportunity of a lifetime when he is hired as a butler at the White House. Over the course of three decades, Cecil has a front-row seat to history and the inner workings of the Oval Office. However, his commitment to his "First Family" leads to tension at home, alienating his wife (Oprah Winfrey) and causing conflict with his anti-establishment son.

---

*Directions: Use what you know and what you see to respond to the following questions/tasks:*

1. Is this movie A. fictional or B. factual?

2. What choice on the map above best describes the geographic location as the movie begins?

3. What is the first year depicted in the movie?
A. 2000
B. 1968
C. 1908
D. 1926
E. none of the choices

4. Was it before or after the Civil War?  A. After  B. Before

5. What happened when Cecil used the "white man's word"?
A. nothing
B. he was slapped
C. he was corrected
D. he was complemented
E. none of the choices

6. Where did Cecil end up in 1957?
A. North Carolina
B. Georgia
C. Washington, D.C.
D. Mississippi
E. none of the choices

7. How many children did Cecil have?
A. 1
B. 2
C. 3
D. 4
E. none of the choices

8. Who were they talking about around the breakfast table?
A. Huey Newton
B. Malcolm X
C. Emmett Till
D. Dr. King
E. none of the choices

9. Cecil got a huge break when he was hired by the….
A. White House
B. Grand Hotel
C. people at Microsoft
D. Marriott Hotel
E. none of the choices

10. Who was the head butler?
A. Randolph Hearst
B. James Holloway
C. Cecil Gains
D. Carter Wilson
E. none of the choices

11. What administration was the first served by Cecil Gains?
A. Kennedy
B. Eisenhower
C. Johnson
D. Carter
E. none of the choices

12. What year was it?
A. 1953
B. 1977
C. 1957
D. 1963
E. none of the choices

13. Did the Gains family have a color TV?   A. Yes   or   B. No

14. Why did President Eisenhower send federal troops to Little Rock, Arkansas?
A. to integrate Central High School
B. to end slavery
C. to enforce segregation
D. to end a riot
E. none of the choices

15. What college did Cecil's son, Louis, attend?
A. Tuskegee
B. Hampton
C. Howard
D. Fisk
E. none of the choices

16. The vice president came down to speak with the butlers. Who was the Vice President?
A. Richard M. Nixon
B. Ronald Reagan
C. Lyndon Johnson
D. John F. Kennedy
E. none of the choices

17. What year does Louis start college?
A. 1953
B. 1977
C. 1960
D. 1963
E. none of the choices

18. Louis participated in what part of the Civil Rights movement?
A. March on Washington
B. Lunch Counter Sit-ins
C. Selma to Montgomery March
D. Montgomery Bus Boycott
E. none of the choices

---

end day 1 - 45:21

# The Butler (Rated PG-13) Day 2

After leaving the South as a young man and finding employment at an elite hotel in Washington, D.C., Cecil Gaines (Forest Whitaker) gets the opportunity of a lifetime when he is hired as a butler at the White House. Over the course of three decades, Cecil has a front-row seat to history and the inner workings of the Oval Office. However, his commitment to his "First Family" leads to tension at home, alienating his wife (Oprah Winfrey) and causing conflict with his anti-establishment son.

---

*Directions: Use what you know and what you see to respond to the following questions/tasks:*

---

1. What administration was the second served by Cecil Gains?
   A. Kennedy
   B. Eisenhower
   C. Johnson
   D. Carter
   E. none of the choices

2. What year was it?
   A. 1953
   B. 1977
   C. 1961
   D. 1963
   E. none of the choices

3. What choice best describes a "freedom ride"?
A. the newest thrill-seeking ride at Cedar Point
B. the crossing of the Atlantic by Europeans to escape religious prosecution
C. the name of the speech given by Dr. King while in Detroit
D. civil rights activists who tested a court ruling that justified that segregation of interstate transportation facilities, including bus terminals, was unconstitutional
E. none of the choices

4. Read the following passage:

> On May 14, 1961, the Greyhound bus was the first to arrive in Anniston, Alabama. There, an angry mob of about 200 white people surrounded the bus, causing the driver to continue past the bus station. The mob followed the bus in automobiles, and when the tires on the bus blew out, someone threw a bomb into the bus. The Freedom Riders escaped the bus as it burst into flames, only to be brutally beaten by members of the surrounding mob. The second bus, a Trailways vehicle, traveled to Birmingham, Alabama, that day, and those riders were also beaten by an angry white mob, many of whom brandished metal pipes. Birmingham Public Safety Commissioner Bull Connor (1897-1973) stated that, although he knew the Freedom Riders were arriving and violence awaited them, he posted no police protection at the station because it was Mother's Day.

Was the scene mentioned above, portrayed in the movie?    A. Yes    B. No

5. According to the movie, did the Freedom Rides persuade JFK to take action (end discrimination and call for equality/justice)?    A. Yes    B. No

6. What administration was the third served by Cecil Gains?
A. Kennedy
B. Eisenhower
C. Johnson
D. Carter
E. none of the choices

7. What year was it?
A. 1953
B. 1977
C. 1964
D. 1963
E. none of the choices

8. Read the following passage:

On "Bloody Sunday," March 7, 1965, some 600 civil rights marchers headed east out of Selma on U.S. Route 80. They only got as far as the Edmund Pettus Bridge six blocks away, where state and local lawmen attacked them with billy clubs and tear gas and drove them back into Selma.

Was the scene mentioned above portrayed in the movie?    A. Yes    B. No

9. Is this a correct statement? None of the presidents knew that Cecil had a son involved in the Civil Rights Movement   A. Yes   B. No

10. Did Louis Gains work with Dr. Martin Luther King, Jr.?   A. Yes   B. No

11. Everything happened after the assassination of Dr. Martin Luther King, Jr. **except for**:
A. fighting
B. vandalism
C. rioting
D. peace
E. none of the choices

12. What party did Louis become part of after Dr. King's death?
A. Republican
B. Democrat
C. Independent
D. Libertarian
E. none of the choices

end day 2 - 1:24:44

# The Butler (Rated PG-13) Day 3

After leaving the South as a young man and finding employment at an elite hotel in Washington, D.C., Cecil Gaines (Forest Whitaker) gets the opportunity of a lifetime when he is hired as a butler at the White House. Over the course of three decades, Cecil has a front-row seat to history and the inner workings of the Oval Office. However, his commitment to his "First Family" leads to tension at home, alienating his wife (Oprah Winfrey) and causing conflict with his anti-establishment son.

*Directions: Use what you know and what you see to respond to the following questions/tasks:*

1. Is the youngest brother, Charlie, going to fight in Vietnam?   A. Yes   B. No

2. What administration was the fourth served by Cecil Gains?
A. Kennedy
B. Eisenhower
C. Johnson
D. Nixon
E. none of the choices

3. What year was it?
A. 1953
B. 1977
C. 1964
D. 1969
E. none of the choices

4. Was President Nixon (A) for or (B) against the Black Panthers?

5. Did Charlie die in Vietnam?  A.  Yes    B.  No

6. Louis Gains became a politician in the state of…..
A.  Michigan
B.  Georgia
C.  Tennessee
D.  Virginia
E.  none of the choices

7. Who was the last president served by Cecil?
A.  Kennedy
B.  Reagan
C.  Johnson
D.  Carter
E.  none of the choices

8. Do Louis and Cecil every come together again?    A.  Yes   B.  No

9. According to Louis, was President Reagan (A) for or (B) against civil rights?

10. As the movie comes close to an end, who had become president of the United States?
A.  Kennedy
B.  Reagan
C.  Johnson
D.  Obama
E.  none of the choices

## Answer Key: The Butler

| Day #1 | Day #2 | Day #3 |
|---|---|---|
| 1. B<br>2. E<br>3. D<br>4. A<br>5. B<br>6. C<br>7. B<br>8. C<br>9. A<br>10. D<br>11. B<br>12. C<br>13. B<br>14. A<br>15. D<br>16. A<br>17. C<br>18. B | 1. A<br>2. C<br>3. D<br>4. A<br>5. A<br>6. C<br>7. C<br>8. A<br>9. B<br>10. A<br>11. D<br>12. E | 1. A<br>2. D<br>3. D<br>4. B<br>5. A<br>6. C<br>7. B<br>8. A<br>9. B<br>10. D |

# Works Cited:

Movie Reviews and Introductions are from the following sources: "1492:

Conquest of Paradise (1992)." *Movie Review Query Engine*,
    www.mrqe.com/movie_reviews/1492-conquest-of-paradise-m100005830.

"12 Years a Slave." *Eventful*,
    movies.eventful.com/12-years-a-slave-/M0-001-000052106-1#tab-details.

"Lincoln." *Roger Ebert*, Ebert Digital LLC, 7 Nov. 2012,
    www.rogerebert.com/reviews/lincoln-2012.

"Avalon Parent Review." *Parent Previews*, edited by Donna Gustafson, One Choice
    Communications, parentpreviews.com/movie-reviews/review/avalon.

"The Lost Battalion." *IMDb*, www.imdb.com/title/tt0287535/plotsummary. "Battle of

the Argonne Forest - 1918." *Maps of the World*, Compare Infobase,
    www.mapsofworld.com/world-war-i/battle-of-argonne-forest.html.

"The Grapes of Wrath." *City Newspaper*, www.rochestercitynewspaper.com/rochester/the-
    grapes-of-wrath/ Film?oid=2336817.

"A Brief History of the Tuskegee Airmen." *CAF Redtail Squadron*, www.redtail.org/the-
    airmen-a-brief-history/.

"Rescue Dawn." *Eventful*, movies.eventful.com/rescue-dawn-/M0-001-000004574-7.

"Selma." *Midco*, Midcontinent Communications,
    midco.net/movies_channel/info.php?movie_id=140501&tab=My+Theaters.

"Mandela: Long Walk to Freedom." *The Hollywood Reporter*,
    www.hollywoodreporter.com/movie/mandela-long-walk-freedom/cast-crew.

"Lee Daniels' The Butler." *Eventful*,
    movies.eventful.com/lee-daniels-the-butler-/M0-001-000050686-8#tab-details.

***Images and maps have all been selected from the public domain.

www.ingramcontent.com/pod-product-compliance
Lightning Source LLC
Chambersburg PA
CBHW080739230426
43665CB00020B/2797